DORLING KINDERSLEY DK EYEWITNESS GUIDES

BASEBALL

The pitching sequence

Early baseball

Charleston, Arkansas, "town team"

1888 Cincinnati
Reds score-card

Outfielder's glove

Mickey Mantle

Ozzie Smith

Louisville Slugger baseball bat

EYEWITNESS GUIDES

BASEBALL

Written by
JAMES KELLEY

Babe Ruth and Lou Gehrig

Ted Williams's spikes

Home plate collision

1999 Little League World
Series Champions

Biography of Satchel Paige

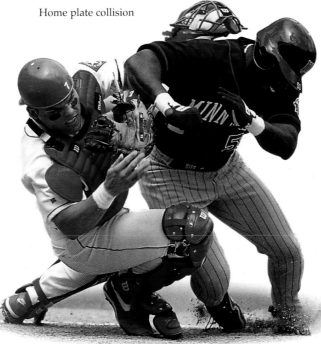

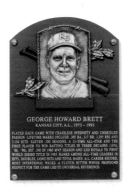

George Brett's
Hall of Fame plaque

Dorling Kindersley

Dorling Kindersley

LONDON, NEW YORK, AUCKLAND, DELHI, JOHANNESBURG,
MUNICH, PARIS and SYDNEY

For a full catalogue, visit

DK www.dk.com

Publisher Neal Porter
Executive Editor Iris Rosoff
Art Director Dirk Kaufman

A Production of the Shoreline Publishing Group
Editorial Director James Buckley, Jr.
Eyewitness Baseball **Designer** Thomas J. Carling
Studio and Memorabilia Photography
Michael Burr and David Spindel

UK Managing Editor Sue Grabham
UK Senior Managing Art Editor Julia Harris
UK Editors Richard Mead, Simon Holland

First published in Great Britain in 2000
by Dorling Kindersley Limited,
9 Henrietta Street, London WC2E 8PS

A CIP catalogue record for this book
is available from the British Library.

ISBN 0 7513 6395 2

Colour reproduction by Colourscan, Singapore
Printed in China by Toppan Printing Co. (Shenzhen) Ltd.

Roger
Clemens

Women's pro
baseball in
the 1940s

World Series trophy

Ken
Griffey, Jr.

1920s
Cleveland
Indians
warm-up
sweater

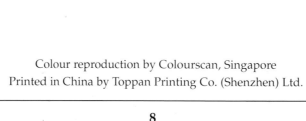

Contents

Hank Aaron

Base ball beginnings

A BALL, A BAT, AND FOUR BASES on a field. The elements of the game that became baseball have been around for hundreds of years, most famously in the English game called "rounders". Americans had been playing another ball game with bases called "town ball" since after the War of Independence. By the 1840s, sportsmen in several Northeastern cities in America were gathering regularly to play several variations of what they called "base ball." In 1845, Alexander Cartwright (inset) and Daniel "Doc" Adams, leaders of the Knickerbocker Base Ball Club, developed the first set of rules for the game. Although those rules changed rapidly over the next few years and continued to evolve into the 1900s, they were close enough to what baseball is today to mark the "birth" of baseball. Since its humble beginnings, the game has grown from a sport played by gentlemen on weekends to a sport played by men, women, boys, and girls of all ages in more than 100 countries.

After going west for the California Gold Rush of 1849, Cartwright later became a fire chief in Honolulu

Diamond and base paths

The author's great-grandfather Nicholas Minden

BATTER UP!
Since the beginning of the game, baseball bats have maintained their unique shape – thick at the top and tapering to a narrower handle. Early bats did not have as much tapering as today's bats, but their function was the same as that described by early baseball hero Willie Keeler – "Meet the ball and hit 'em where they ain't."

Thick handle

Union Army uniform

THE DOUBLEDAY MYTH
A 1911 commission to trace the "official" origin of baseball somehow settled on the story of Union Army General Abner Doubleday, who, it was claimed, invented the game in 1839 in Cooperstown, New York. Modern research has completely disproved this theory, although the "myth" of his involvement remains popular today.

TOWN TEAMS
A key to the growth of baseball across America in the late 1800s was the formation of "town teams," such as this one from Charleston, Arkansas (shown after World War I). The players were amateurs, the sponsors local businessmen, and the prize was the right to brag to neighbouring towns. But many great players started out playing on teams like this one.

Pitcher   *Batter*   *Catcher*

BASEBALL HEADS SOUTH
The Civil War (1861–65) helped spread baseball around America, as Union soldiers took their game, most popular around New York, on the road with them. This noted 1863 lithograph shows Union prisoners at a Confederate camp in Salisbury, North Carolina, putting on a game watched by guards and fellow prisoners alike.

Casey at the Bat

(This is an excerpt from the most famous baseball poem, written in 1888 by Ernest L. Thayer. It tells the story of a fabled player getting one last chance to save the day.)

…Then from 5,000 throats and more there rose a lusty yell;
It rumbled through the valley, it rattled in the dell;
It knocked upon the mountain and recoiled upon the flat,
For Casey, mighty Casey, was advancing to the bat.

There was ease in Casey's manner as he stepped into his place;
There was pride in Casey's bearing and a smile on Casey's face.
And when, responding to the cheers, he lightly doffed his hat,
No stranger in the crowd could doubt 'twas Casey at the bat….

{Several stanzas later…}
…The sneer is gone from Casey's lip, his teeth are clenched in hate;
He pounds with cruel violence his bat upon the plate.
And now the pitcher holds the ball, and now he lets it go,
And now the air is shattered by the force of Casey's blow.

Oh, somewhere in this favoured land the sun is shining bright;
The band is playing somewhere, and somewhere hearts are light,
And somewhere men are laughing, and somewhere children shout;
But there is no joy in Mudville – mighty Casey has struck out.

PLAY BALL!
The first baseballs quickly became soft and mushy as play went on. Players soon learned that winding yarn more tightly around a rubber centre, then covering with tightly stitched leather, made a harder ball that travelled further and lasted longer.

Leather stitching

BASEBALL TUNES
Even bandleader John Philip Sousa (right, in suit) sponsored a team. This song, the "Three Strikes Two-Step," was written in honour of his team. It was one of many tunes, poems (left), and stories about baseball, as it quickly became known in America as the "National Pastime."

Birth of the pros

ALTHOUGH BASEBALL'S BEGINNINGS WERE HUMBLE, it did not take long for players to realize there was a way to make money playing this game. By the years after the Civil War, top players were being lured from club to club by secret payments. In 1869, the Cincinnati Red Stockings dropped the pretence and announced themselves as professional players. They ruled the East, playing (and defeating) all challengers. Two years later, the National Association joined together several pro teams to form the first pro league. From then on, baseball was to have two worlds, the professionals and everyone else. In the late 19th century, several pro leagues rose and fell. By 1901, there were two "major leagues," along with several other "minor" pro leagues, much as it is today.

SPALDING'S SPORT
Albert G. Spalding was a top-notch pitcher in his youth, achieving an amazing 57–5 won/lost record in 1875. He also helped create the National League in 1876, was later president of the Chicago White Sox, and led a world baseball tour in 1888. He also founded the still thriving Spalding Sporting Goods Company.

High-button shoes worn for photo, not for games

Championship medal

EARLY CHAMPS
The Baltimore Base Ball Club won the 1894 National League championship. Using a style of baseball known as "little ball," they were led by the famously fierce player-manager John McGraw.

PRE-WORLD SERIES
The World Series would not begin until 1903, but teams saw the benefit of post-season tournaments early on. From 1894-97, the first- and second-placed teams in the National League played each other for the Temple Cup. In 1896 (right), the Baltimore Orioles finished first in the league, and also won the Cup with four straight victories over Cleveland.

EARLY OUTFITS
Early pro players enjoyed snappy outfits as much as today's players do. This heavy wool warm-up sweater was sported by members of the Cleveland Indians, one of the first teams in the American League.

FOR THE FANS
The growth of pro teams, such as the American Association's Cincinnati Reds (featuring 27–14 pitcher Lee Viau in 1888, below), led to the creation of numerous score-cards, programmes, magazines, and souvenirs that fans used to follow their new favourite teams and players.

Thick ribbed wool

Take Me Out To the Ball Game

(Written in 1908 by Jack Norworth and Albert Von Tilzer, this song is sung at every baseball game during the top and bottom of the seventh inning – the seventh-inning stretch.)

Take me out to the ball game,
Take me out with the crowd.
Buy me some peanuts and Cracker Jack,
I don't care if I never get back.

So it's root, root, root for the home team.
If they don't win, it's a shame!
For it's one, two, three strikes you're out,
At the Old Ball Game!

Filed July 31 1869

FIRST NINE OF THE

CINCINNATI

(RED STOCKINGS) BASE BALL CLUB.

Harry Wright

THE FIRST PROS

Harry Wright, captain and founder of the 1869 Cincinnati Red Stockings (left), the first all-professional team, has been called the "father of pro baseball." Along with starting the Red Stockings, Wright invented the basic baseball kit still used today and patented the first score-card. He guided his team to an 18-month winning streak, and later led Boston's entry into the new National Association, in 1871.

Note spelling of "Base Ball"

ON THE ROAD

By the turn of the century, pro baseball had spread as far west as Chicago and St. Louis and as far south as Louisville. This schedule (above) from 1899 also shows the Reds making stops in Washington, Philadelphia, New York, and "Pittsburg," as it used to be spelt.

FINALLY. . .SAFETY

Early catchers wore little or no safety equipment. Spurred on by the professional game, the first catchers' masks were developed in the 1870s. This example is from near the turn of the century. It would not be until the years before World War I that catchers regularly began using chest protectors and shin guards.

Iron bars

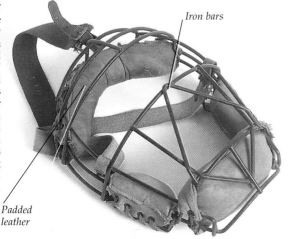

Padded leather

Webbing was simple leather strip

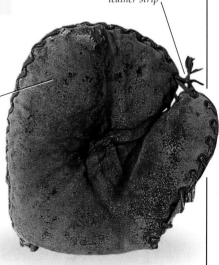

Early padded first baseman's glove

GLOVES ON FIRST

First basemen were the first players apart from catchers to regularly use gloves Having to catch numerous hard throws throughout a game led to the development of this thickly padded mitt. Its flimsy "webbing" was a far cry from today's big, basket-like gloves.

The Babe

WITHOUT QUESTION, George Herman "Babe" Ruth is the most famous and important baseball player in history. It would be hard to overestimate the impact the Babe had on the game, both as a player and symbol. His statistics are known as "Ruthian," a word that today still conjures up both the might of his sweeping swing and his larger-than-life personality. In 22 seasons (1914–35), the Sultan of Swat slugged 714 home runs. To put that into context, the previous career record holder had 138. When he hit 54 home runs for the Yankees in 1920, his total was more than nearly every other *team's*, and 25 more than the previous record – set by the Bambino himself in 1919. His best single-season total – 60 home runs in 1927 – was a record for 34 years. Every home run hitter – and every world-famous athlete in any sport – competes with the legend of the Babe. It is a battle they cannot win.

Ruth used an unusually large 1.2 kg (2.6 lbs) bat

Officially listed at 97 kg, Ruth often weighed much more

WHAT MIGHT HAVE BEEN
With Boston from 1914-19, young Babe Ruth was one of baseball's best pitchers. But Red Sox owner Harry Frazee sold Ruth to the New York Yankees in 1919, forever saddling the Red Sox with the "Curse of the Bambino."

A POWERFUL PAIR
Ruth and Lou Gehrig (right) were team-mates on the Yankees for 13 years, helping New York win four World Series. Here they are shown in kits worn during an off-season exhibition tour. Gehrig was nearly Ruth's equal as a batter. His career was cut short by the muscle illness that today bears his name.

"Larrupin'" was slang for "slugging"

Ruth first got number three because he batted third. Kit numbers were not regularly used until the 1920s

THE "CALLED SHOT"
This statuette of Ruth, showing his famous number 3, recalls one of baseball's most controversial moments. In the 1932 World Series, did Ruth point to the centrefield seats right before he slugged a homer there? Or was he waving at the heckling by Cubs' players?

Babe Ruth Pays No Tax On His Size
He-s A Giant in Physique, Still His Royal Clothes Cost Nothing Extra On That Account

AN ADVERTISING BABE
Ruth's incredible popularity led to his earning big money (at the time) for endorsements such as this one for large-size men's clothes.

Note the high socks, the style of the times

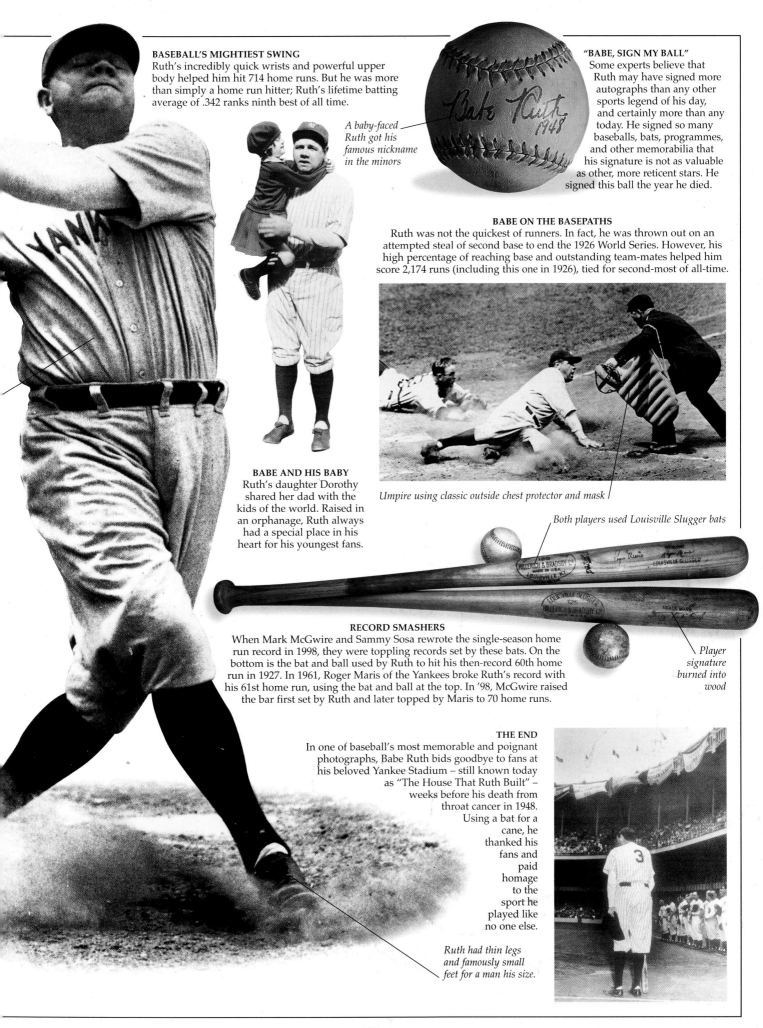

BASEBALL'S MIGHTIEST SWING
Ruth's incredibly quick wrists and powerful upper body helped him hit 714 home runs. But he was more than simply a home run hitter; Ruth's lifetime batting average of .342 ranks ninth best of all time.

A baby-faced Ruth got his famous nickname in the minors

"BABE, SIGN MY BALL"
Some experts believe that Ruth may have signed more autographs than any other sports legend of his day, and certainly more than any today. He signed so many baseballs, bats, programmes, and other memorabilia that his signature is not as valuable as other, more reticent stars. He signed this ball the year he died.

BABE ON THE BASEPATHS
Ruth was not the quickest of runners. In fact, he was thrown out on an attempted steal of second base to end the 1926 World Series. However, his high percentage of reaching base and outstanding team-mates helped him score 2,174 runs (including this one in 1926), tied for second-most of all-time.

BABE AND HIS BABY
Ruth's daughter Dorothy shared her dad with the kids of the world. Raised in an orphanage, Ruth always had a special place in his heart for his youngest fans.

Umpire using classic outside chest protector and mask

Both players used Louisville Slugger bats

RECORD SMASHERS
When Mark McGwire and Sammy Sosa rewrote the single-season home run record in 1998, they were toppling records set by these bats. On the bottom is the bat and ball used by Ruth to hit his then-record 60th home run in 1927. In 1961, Roger Maris of the Yankees broke Ruth's record with his 61st home run, using the bat and ball at the top. In '98, McGwire raised the bar first set by Ruth and later topped by Maris to 70 home runs.

Player signature burned into wood

THE END
In one of baseball's most memorable and poignant photographs, Babe Ruth bids goodbye to fans at his beloved Yankee Stadium – still known today as "The House That Ruth Built" – weeks before his death from throat cancer in 1948. Using a bat for a cane, he thanked his fans and paid homage to the sport he played like no one else.

Ruth had thin legs and famously small feet for a man his size.

The Major Leagues

Arizona Diamondbacks

Atlanta Braves

Chicago Cubs

Cincinnati Reds

Colorado Rockies

Florida Marlins

Houston Astros

Los Angeles Dodgers

Milwaukee Brewers

Montreal Expos

American League

Anaheim Angels

THE BEST BASEBALL in the world is played by the 30 teams that make up Major League Baseball. The Majors have two parts – the 16-team National League, formed in 1876, and the 14-team American League, which started to play in 1901. Several A.L. teams, including the Boston Red Sox, Detroit Tigers, Chicago White Sox, and Cleveland Indians, remain in the cities in which they first played. The Chicago Cubs and Cincinnati Reds survive from the earliest days of the N.L. Over the decades, many teams have moved, taken on new nicknames, or been added to the Majors. Today, Major League teams are found from coast to coast. Two even play in Canada (the Montreal Expos and Toronto Blue Jays). All this geography does not begin to describe the impact of the Majors on American life and sports culture. The continuity of the game – as played at its highest level in the Majors – helped to define the course of the 20th century.

THE GREAT GRIFFEY
Seattle Mariners outfielder Ken Griffey, Jr., is perhaps the best all-round player in the Major Leagues today. Since joining the Mariners at the age of 19, in 1989 – when he made history by sharing the outfield with his father, Ken Griffey, Sr. – "Junior" has combined power (six seasons of 40 or more home runs) with a high batting average (.300 for his career) and a nine-year string of Gold Gloves for fielding excellence. Many observers think he will someday take his place among baseball's all-time greatest players.

Baseball cap with team logo

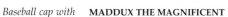

MADDUX THE MAGNIFICENT
Pitcher Greg Maddux of the Atlanta Braves does not overpower hitters, and he looks about as menacing as the ice cream man. But he gets batters out better than almost any other pitcher in baseball history. Maddux was the dominant National League pitcher of the 1990s, winning four Cy Young Awards and finishing in the top four in the voting on two other occasions. Each year since 1990, Maddux has also won the Gold Glove for pitchers, awarded for fielding excellence.

FUN FOR THE FANS
While a Major League Baseball game is a great show on the field, many teams add to the entertainment for fans with promotions, giveaways, and mascots – such as Philadelphia's "Phillie Phanatic" (left). The coolest way to get a souvenir is to catch a foul ball hit into the stands (above).

New York Mets

Philadelphia Phillies

Pittsburgh Pirates

St. Louis Cardinals

San Diego Padres

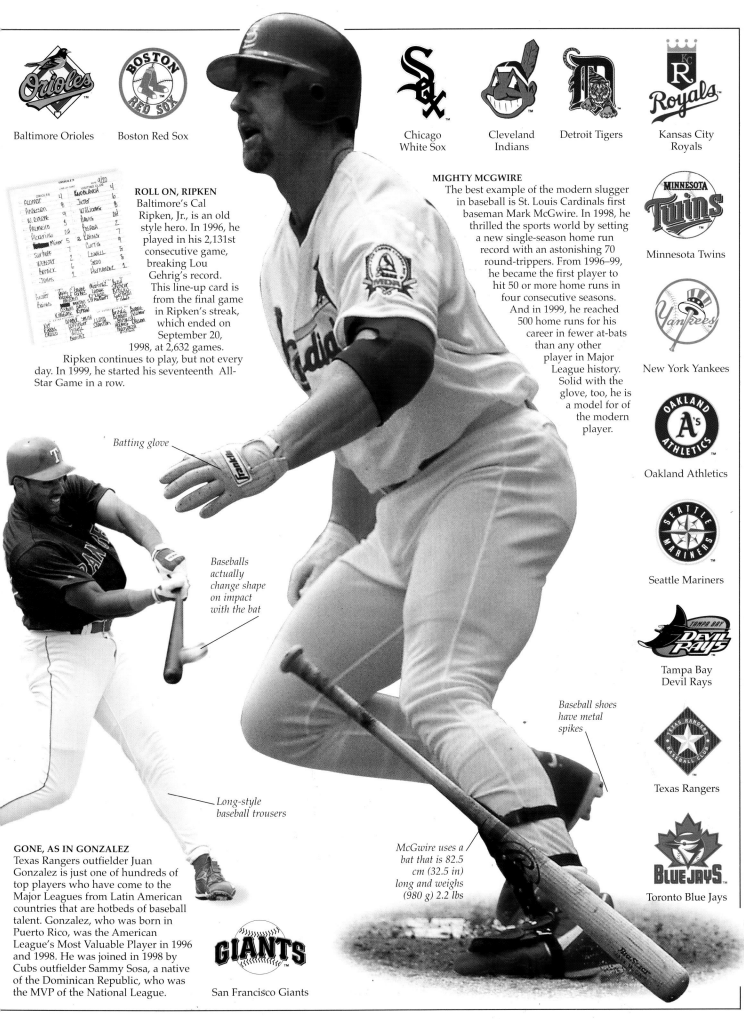

Baltimore Orioles

Boston Red Sox

Chicago White Sox

Cleveland Indians

Detroit Tigers

Kansas City Royals

ROLL ON, RIPKEN

Baltimore's Cal Ripken, Jr., is an old style hero. In 1996, he played in his 2,131st consecutive game, breaking Lou Gehrig's record. This line-up card is from the final game in Ripken's streak, which ended on September 20, 1998, at 2,632 games. Ripken continues to play, but not every day. In 1999, he started his seventeenth All-Star Game in a row.

MIGHTY MCGWIRE

The best example of the modern slugger in baseball is St. Louis Cardinals first baseman Mark McGwire. In 1998, he thrilled the sports world by setting a new single-season home run record with an astonishing 70 round-trippers. From 1996–99, he became the first player to hit 50 or more home runs in four consecutive seasons. And in 1999, he reached 500 home runs for his career in fewer at-bats than any other player in Major League history. Solid with the glove, too, he is a model for of the modern player.

Minnesota Twins

New York Yankees

Oakland Athletics

Seattle Mariners

Tampa Bay Devil Rays

Texas Rangers

Toronto Blue Jays

Batting glove

Baseballs actually change shape on impact with the bat

Baseball shoes have metal spikes

Long-style baseball trousers

McGwire uses a bat that is 82.5 cm (32.5 in) long and weighs (980 g) 2.2 lbs

GONE, AS IN GONZALEZ

Texas Rangers outfielder Juan Gonzalez is just one of hundreds of top players who have come to the Major Leagues from Latin American countries that are hotbeds of baseball talent. Gonzalez, who was born in Puerto Rico, was the American League's Most Valuable Player in 1996 and 1998. He was joined in 1998 by Cubs outfielder Sammy Sosa, a native of the Dominican Republic, who was the MVP of the National League.

GIANTS

San Francisco Giants

The diamond

IF BASEBALL DIAMONDS were any other size, baseball would probably not work. But a baseball diamond is exactly 90 feet on each side – that is, the distance from one base to the next is 27.43 m (exactly 90 feet). So each ground ball hit to the shortstop means a close play at first base. Each double play is turned as quickly as possible, and the time it takes a base stealer to go from first base to second base is just about the time it takes a pitcher to pitch and a catcher to throw down to second. Of course, a purist might note that a baseball diamond is actually a square viewed from one corner. But the shape is close enough that, at the infield area came to be called a diamond and soon the entire baseball field was known by this name. Beyond the base paths is the dirt infield area; beyond this, the grass (or artificial turf) outfield area. The outfield fences define the back of the field, while the foul lines extending from home plate define the sides. A diamond is much more than lines, fences, and bases, however. A baseball diamond is the place where dreams come true.

DIAMONDS OF OLD
This photo of Griffith Stadium, Washington DC – from 1933 shows that diamonds have not changed much from earlier times. A wide dirt area separated the infield grass from the outfield grass. This view also shows the netting that ballparks put up behind the home plate to protect fans from fast-moving foul balls or wild pitches.

Outfield fences, usually padded

Outfield bleachers

Left field

FAIR OR FOUL?
At the outfield end of the two foul lines are tall "foul poles." Any ball hit to the field side of the pole is fair; a ball to the outside of the pole is foul. Any ball that hits the foul pole is, ironically, fair. Most foul poles have nets (below) attached to the field side of the pole to help umpires make their calls.

Left field foul line

Third base

Third base coach's box

ON THE DIAMOND
The geometry of baseball and the diamond on which it is played makes the game unique. The white foul lines stretch out into the outfield, while imaginary lines define the paths between first, second, and third bases. Many teams cut their outfield grass in geometric patterns to create a more pleasing picture for audiences watching both at the park and at home on television.

A BALL CLUB'S SECOND HOME

The area where baseball teams sit during games, when they are not on the field, is called the dugout. Normally, dugouts are located at or below the level of the playing surface. Players wait on the bench for their turn to bat or rest between innings in the field. In the dugout, players also receive refreshments, discuss strategy with their coaches, and cheer on their team-mates. In most stadiums, the dugouts lead directly to the locker rooms, where the teams change before the game and shower afterwards.

PATH TO THE PLATE

This photo from the 1930s shows two things now only rarely seen on diamonds and at ballparks – a dirt path between the pitcher's mound and home plate (today only Arizona's Bank One Ballpark has this old-time look) and seats with an obstructed view. Fans unfortunate enough to sit behind the steel beam upright (centre) would have a hard time seeing some plays. Modern stadiums are all constructed without such obstructions.

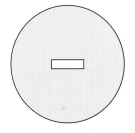

AT THE CENTRE

At the centre of every diamond's infield is the pitcher's mound. Rules call for it to be 5.5m (18 ft) in diameter and 25 cm (10 in) above the level of home plate. The pitching rubber measures 61 cm by 15 cm (24 in by 6 in) and is 18.44 m (60.5 ft) from home plate. A pitcher must be touching the rubber to begin each pitch.

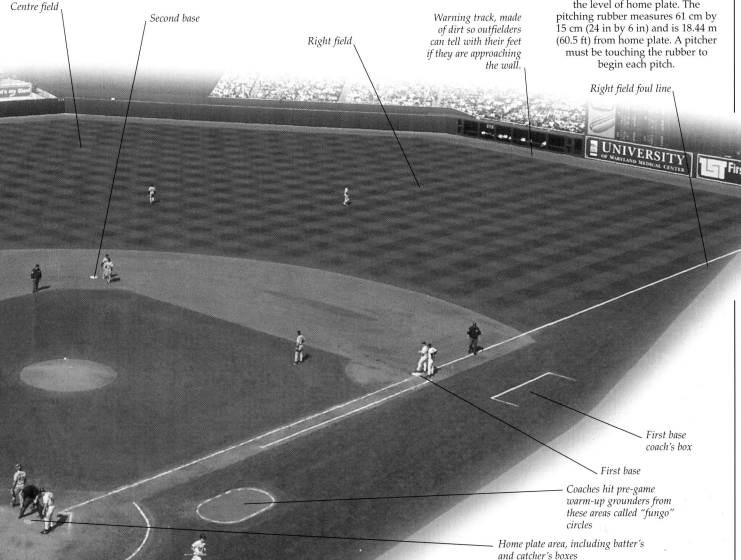

Centre field

Second base

Right field

Warning track, made of dirt so outfielders can tell with their feet if they are approaching the wall.

Right field foul line

First base coach's box

First base

Coaches hit pre-game warm-up grounders from these areas called "fungo" circles

Home plate area, including batter's and catcher's boxes

Bats and balls

Take a stick, the lumber, a wand, or a toothpick. Combine it with a pearl, an apple, a pill, a rock, or a pea. What have you got? Everything you need to play baseball. Baseball bats and baseballs have earned many nicknames in the 150 years since the game began to become popular. Whilst many things have changed, the idea of hitting a round ball with a long, rounded stick has remained the same. The bats and balls used by Major League stars over the years have also become more than just the tools of their trade – they have become legends in their own right, collected and treasured by generations of fans. Bats used by great players are housed in the Baseball Hall of Fame. Signed baseballs reside by the thousands on the shelves of fans all around the world. The ball that Mark McGwire hit for his 70th home run in 1998 sold to a private collector for £1,875,000 ($3 million). A pearl of great price, you might say.

The signature of the appropriate league president is printed on the ball

WHAT THE PROS USE

Since 1975, the American and National Leagues have used this cow-leather-covered ball produced by Rawlings. Before then, the ball was covered with horsehide and made by Spalding. Home teams have to supply five dozen new balls for every regular season game. Umpires or clubhouse personnel "rub them up" with a special compound to take off the shine created in the factory..

FROM TREE TO BAT

The most famous example of a wooden bat used in the Majors is the Louisville Slugger, made by the Hillerich & Bradsby Company in Louisville, Kentucky. To make a bat, a Northern white ash tree – at least sixty years old – is cut down. Trees less than 30 cm (12 in) in diameter are cut into long pieces ("split"). From the centre of the split, the "square" is rip-sawed. On a lathe, the square becomes a round cylinder. On another lathe, the bat is roughly shaped (note the extra pieces on the ends that hold the bat in place). In the next stage, the bat is sanded smooth. The finished product (below) has been dipped in black lacquer (not all bats are dipped) and then foil branded with the company's famous logo as well as the player's signature.

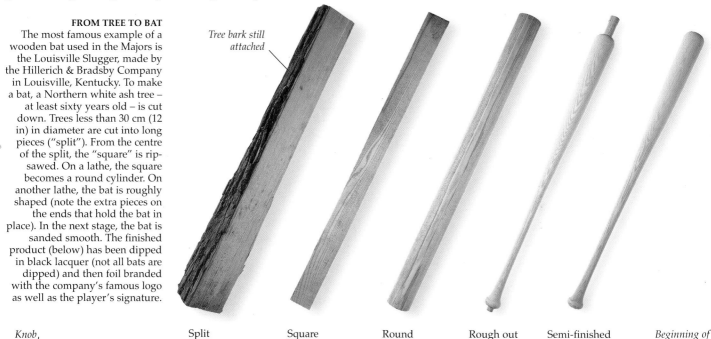

Tree bark still attached

Split   Square   Round   Rough out   Semi-finished   *Beginning of barrel*

Knob

Handle

INSIDE THE BASEBALL

Not every baseball is made like this one, but this is the baseball used at the highest level of play in the world – the Major Leagues. Official balls must weigh between 142 g and 149 g (0.31–0.33 lb). They must have a circumference of between 22.9 cm and 23.5 cm (9–9.25 in). The life-span of a Major League baseball during a game is about six pitches. Home team personnel supply new balls as required to the home plate umpire to put into play.

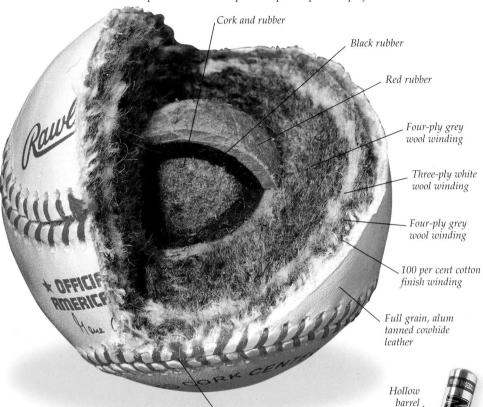

Cork and rubber

Black rubber

Red rubber

Four-ply grey wool winding

Three-ply white wool winding

Four-ply grey wool winding

100 per cent cotton finish winding

Full grain, alum tanned cowhide leather

Five-ply waxed cotton thread, hand-stitched

Player's uniform number

THE BOTTLE BAT
Heinie Groh, who played for the Cincinnati Reds from 1912–1921, was the only player to successfully use this strange form of bat. Unlike normal bats, which taper, it was thinner at the handle and uniformly wide along the barrel.

AT THE BAT RACK
Baseball players take good care of their most important offensive tool – their bat. During the game, players store several bats in the bat rack in the dugout. A player might have half a dozen bats at the ready, in case one breaks during the game. Before the season, players receive large shipments of bats made to their specifications; more can be ordered if necessary.

IT GOES PING
The development of the aluminium bat in the early 1970s changed baseball at every level except the professional. Much sturdier than wood bats, aluminium bats last much longer and are almost impossible to break. Youth leagues, schools and colleges learned to love the cost efficiency of the aluminium bat. Purists bemoan its odd sound, and the effect aluminium has on batters. What would be outs with wood are singles with aluminium; what would be fly outs with wood are home runs. Still, today more players use aluminium than wood.

Hollow barrel

Signature of Ken Griffey, Jr. H&B has thousands of cards on file with the bat preferences of Major Leaguers

BALLPARK DOUGHNUTS
While warming up before hitting, some players slip this weighted ring, called a "doughnut," onto their bat. It fits over the knob but not the barrel. Swinging the bat with this added weight makes swinging the bat without it seem easier and quicker.

Baseball gloves

WHILST MANY THINGS ABOUT BASEBALL have remained almost the same since the first games were played, one piece of equipment – the baseball glove – has undergone many changes. In fact, gloves were not even regularly used by players (left) until the late 1800s. Even then, only the catcher wore one, and it was not much more than a leather glove with a bit of padding in the palm. Gloves, or mitts, as they are also called, evolved slowly as more players began using them. The fingers were stitched together. The space between the thumb and forefinger was widened, creating a basket or pocket. The fingers got longer, the better to stop line drives. The leather got looser and more pliable, making the glove more comfortable, and mitts became more specialized for each position. No matter how big or wide or hi-tech a baseball glove is, it is only as useful as the hand that is inside it. A glove will not catch a ball all by itself.

Webbing

Pocket

Thumb

Early gloves had little webbing

Fingers not laced together

IN THE OLD DAYS
Early gloves, such as this one from the 1920s, offered players little padding compared to today's gloves, and virtually no additional reach. Today's players usually snag the ball in the web between the thumb and forefinger. Players back then had to grasp the ball to their palm with their fingers to catch it, rather than cradling it in the webbing.

LITTLE MITTS
Mitts for younger players are the same style as those for Major Leaguers, except they are smaller. Players young and old use their mitts to field grounders, as this infielder demonstrates. The glove's lacing and webbing create a wide "scoop" that makes this task easier.

JUST LIKE MICKEY
Major League players have long endorsed mitts, whether a replica of the model they use themselves or a child-sized souvenir model like this one from the 1960s. Note the differences between the earlier model (above left) and this one, with the fingers stitched together, and much wider webbing between thumb and forefinger. Even so, the fingers were still not much bigger than on the hand.

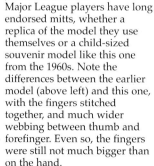

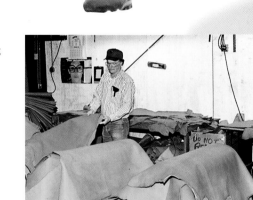

Laces holding fingers together

Laces holding pieces of glove together

GOLD GLOVES
Since 1957, Major League players who excel with their gloves (and their throwing arms) are awarded the Gold Glove (left). There is one winner for every position in each league (three outfielders are chosen in each league). Giants centre fielder Willie Mays earned 12 consecutive Gold Gloves, including this one, from 1957–68.

CATCHER'S MITT
Among the most specialized of baseball gloves are those used by catchers. Features include extra padding in the pocket, an extra-wide webbing (right), and an adjustable strap to ensure a tight and comfortable fit. This particular glove is made with two colours of leather. Some choose to use one colour, usually brown or black.

Model name

PITCHER'S GLOVE
A key to a pitcher's glove is secrecy. Pitchers use their gloves to hide until the last minute the grip they are using on the ball, so they don't give hitters any clue as to what they are throwing. While some outfielders' gloves have open webbing, pitchers always use gloves with closed webbing.

Finger sleeve

Heel

BIG BASKET AT FIRST
After the catcher's glove, the first baseman's glove is the most unique. These gloves are longer and thinner than outfield gloves. They are more pointed at the top, the better to scoop low throws out of the dirt or to stretch out for throws that are off-line. First basemen learn to make catches that create an audible "pop" when the ball hits the mitt. Umpires often listen for the sound while watching the base for the runner's foot.

GLOVE STORY
This typical outfielder's glove shows many of the features that make today's gloves so much better than baseball's first mitts. The large, secure webbing between the thumb and forefinger helps trap the ball; it is where most of the catches are made. The longer fingers help players reach for balls hit or thrown to the side or over their heads. Padding in the heel and in the fingers helps cushion hard-hit balls. In addition, specially chosen leather (left) makes each glove a soft and cushiony basket for making great catches.

Hats and helmets

Crown

THEY ARE CALLED BASEBALL CAPS, but golfers wear them on the golf course, race car drivers wear them after races, and American football quarterbacks and coaches wear them on the touch-line. These days, it seems as if everyone in the non-sports world is wearing them, too. Baseball caps are the game's most important contribution to fashion. Whilst baseball players wear caps for team identity and to keep the sun out of their eyes, many other pursuits have adopted the distinctive crown and brim of a baseball cap for use in their own sports. Major League players wear very durable, high-quality hats fitted to each player's head. When you are in the big leagues, you do not have to deal with those plastic clips at the back of your cap. As for baseball helmets, they are a much more recent addition to the game. Although a few players tried some form of helmet in the game's early years, it was only after the development of hard plastic during World War II that a durable and comfortable helmet could be made. Today, baseball players at all levels must wear helmets to protect their heads while batting.

EXTRA PROTECTION
Many youth leagues now insist that batters wear face guards, such as this one, along with plastic batting helmets with ear flaps on both sides. Face guards are designed to protect a batter's face from both pitches and foul tips, whilst also allowing good visibility. Although they can be awkward and uncomfortable, they can also be very helpful, especially to inexperienced players looking for confidence at the plate.

Hard plastic, usually in team colour

Ear hole

CHANGING TIMES
Just as styles in fashion change through time, so, too, do caps change in baseball. Although a few teams have left their cap styles unchanged, these Baltimore Orioles' caps show how teams have changed the colours, logos, and design throughout the years. In addition, this is a great way to sell more souvenir caps, as fans try to keep up with their heroes.

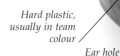

Team logo patch

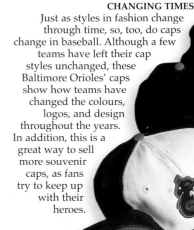

EARLY MAJOR LEAGUE HELMETS
The first helmets used in the Major Leagues were little more than hard plastic versions of the baseball cap, as modelled here by Minnesota Twins slugger Harmon Killebrew (who hit 574 home runs during his career). These helmets had little padding and afforded little protection.

Orioles' logo

SAFETY ON TOP
Although plastic batting helmets have been around since the 1950s, it was only in 1971 that wearing them became mandatory in the Major Leagues. Pro players can wear models with only one ear flap (facing the pitcher), while players at other levels wear helmets with two ear flaps. The reason for batting helmets is simple. Being hit in the head with a pitch can be very dangerous. Many players' careers have been shortened after such "beanballs," as they are called. Only one Major League player has died as a result of being "beaned" – Ray Chapman in 1920. Today's players are better protected.

Strap attached rubber device to cap

Brim

AN UNPOPULAR FIRST TRY
Players in early baseball did not have the advantage of plastic. One enterprising company tried to market this air-filled rubber device as a helmet. It attached to the player's cap with an elastic strap. It was ineffective and did not catch on.

A MOST TRADITIONAL TOPPER
At no matter what level a player competes, from the junior leagues to the Majors, he or she wears a baseball cap on the field. Baseball caps are as much about tradition as function. They keep the sun out of a player's eyes, but what do they do at night? Or in an indoor stadium? Wearing the traditional cap is as much a part of being a ballplayer as swinging a bat. Caps are normally made of six triangular panels held together by a fabric-covered, galvanized steel button at the top. The team logo is on the front of the cap.

Foam padding

Snap for chin stud, sometimes used in youth baseball.

Ventilation holes

FROM THE OLD DAYS
This New York Giants cap from 1922 shows that baseball caps have changed only slightly over the years. The primary changes have come in the height of the crown and the width of the brim. Early caps were worn more snugly on the top of the head, and the brims were a bit shorter.

Brim, usually fabric stitched over heavy cardboard

Baseball kits

Fitted cap

Year made (1952), chest size (46), player's number (9)

THE MAIN REASON FOR KITS IS SIMPLE – to tell who is on which team. Baseball kits are designed to allow freedom of movement and comfort as the player plays the game. Imitating the first examples, today's kit consists of a short-sleeved shirt (often worn over a longer-sleeved undershirt), trousers with a belt, and a baseball cap. Now, baseball kits are made of tight-fitting, stretchy polyester and other synthetic fabrics. Early kits were made of heavy wool that got heavier as the game progressed and the player sweated. Baseball trousers have always been a unique feature in sport. They are supposed to stop just below the knee, as they did until the last decade. But today's fashion-conscious Major Leaguers almost always prefer much longer trousers, even though this goes against tradition. Unfortunately, these longer trousers hide another unique part of the baseball kit – stirrup socks worn over white socks. As with any baseball equipment, the kit is not as important as what the player does while he is wearing it.

SUPERSTAR SHIRT AND SHOES
Each team has a unique design on its jerseys. This home Red Sox jersey belonged to the great Ted Williams. Boston has not changed its basic logo for decades, but other teams have changed their looks and logos several times. Williams's baseball shoes (below) show that the basic configuration of the metal spikes (three-pronged triangles at front and back) has not changed much since the "Splendid Splinter," as he was known, wore these in the 1950s.

Leather uppers

Metal spikes tacked to soles

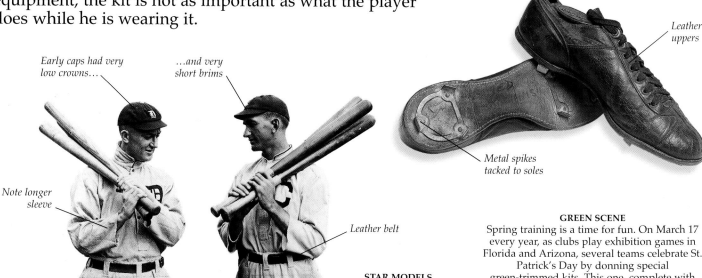

Early caps had very low crowns…

…and very short brims

Note longer sleeve

Leather belt

Trousers fall to just below knees

High socks, before stirrups

STAR MODELS
Detroit's Hall of Fame outfielder Ty Cobb (left) and "Shoeless" Joe Jackson of the Chicago White Sox model kits worn in the Majors before World War I. Compare the baggy wool trousers and jerseys to the sleek, tight-fitting kits of today's players. The thick wool of the kits made keeping them clean difficult, and they were almost permanently stained with grass and dirt.

GREEN SCENE
Spring training is a time for fun. On March 17 every year, as clubs play exhibition games in Florida and Arizona, several teams celebrate St. Patrick's Day by donning special green-trimmed kits. This one, complete with shamrock on the sleeve, was worn by Hall of Fame pitcher Tom Seaver when he was with the Cincinnati Reds. For one day each spring, the team becomes the Cincinnati Greens.

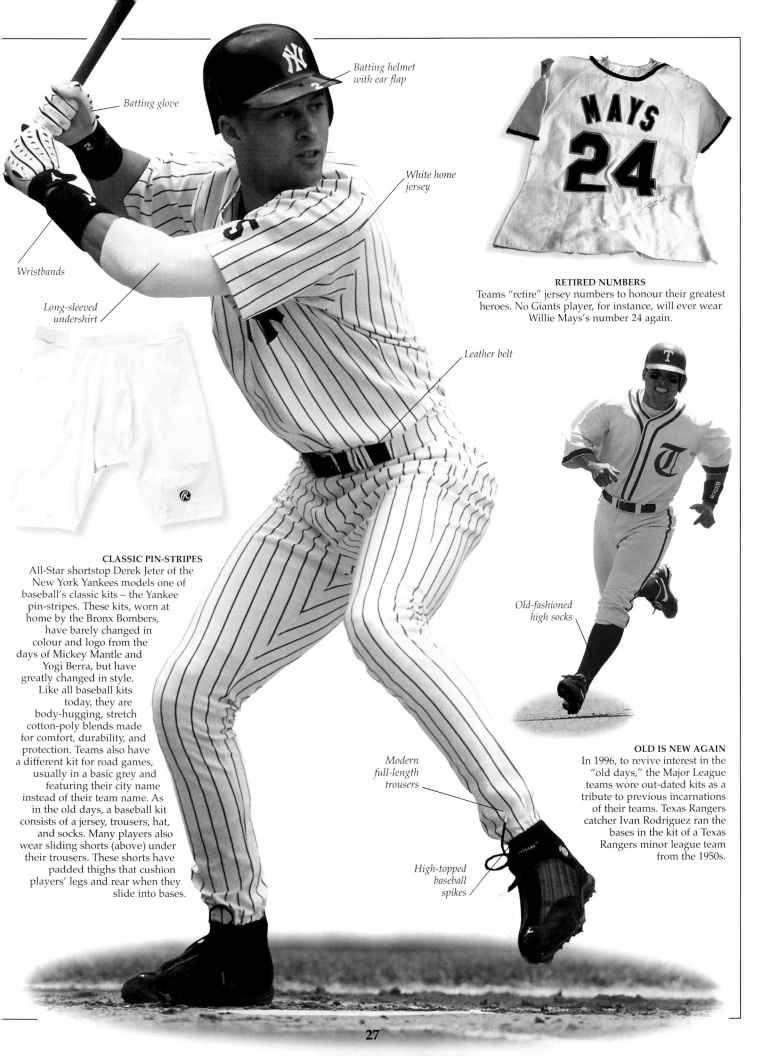

Batting glove

Batting helmet with ear flap

Wristbands

White home jersey

Long-sleeved undershirt

Leather belt

RETIRED NUMBERS
Teams "retire" jersey numbers to honour their greatest heroes. No Giants player, for instance, will ever wear Willie Mays's number 24 again.

MAYS
24

CLASSIC PIN-STRIPES
All-Star shortstop Derek Jeter of the New York Yankees models one of baseball's classic kits – the Yankee pin-stripes. These kits, worn at home by the Bronx Bombers, have barely changed in colour and logo from the days of Mickey Mantle and Yogi Berra, but have greatly changed in style. Like all baseball kits today, they are body-hugging, stretch cotton-poly blends made for comfort, durability, and protection. Teams also have a different kit for road games, usually in a basic grey and featuring their city name instead of their team name. As in the old days, a baseball kit consists of a jersey, trousers, hat, and socks. Many players also wear sliding shorts (above) under their trousers. These shorts have padded thighs that cushion players' legs and rear when they slide into bases.

Old-fashioned high socks

Modern full-length trousers

High-topped baseball spikes

OLD IS NEW AGAIN
In 1996, to revive interest in the "old days," the Major League teams wore out-dated kits as a tribute to previous incarnations of their teams. Texas Rangers catcher Ivan Rodriguez ran the bases in the kit of a Texas Rangers minor league team from the 1950s.

Pitching

Two-seam fastball

Curveball

"Circle" change-up

Knuckleball

GETTING A GRIP
Different pitches are thrown using different grips (above). Pitchers determine how a ball moves or curves by changing the position of their fingers on the raised seams of the ball, or by turning their wrist.

THE PITCHER'S MOUND is the centre of the baseball universe. Nothing happens in a baseball game until the pitcher starts his wind-up and fires in that first pitch. His job is to get the opposing hitters out, but saying that and doing it are two very different things. Warren Spahn (363 wins, the most by a left-hander) said, "Hitting is the art of timing. Pitching is the art of upsetting timing." A wide variety of pitching styles (left) is used to upset a hitter's timing. An even wider variety of arm motions, leg movements, and body spins has also been put to use over the years. Until the 1930s, pitchers could legally deface a ball, either by cutting it or applying all sorts of "foreign substances" (including spit) to make it harder to hit. It is a tough job – pitchers need all the help they can get.

Pitchers focus their eyes on their target – the catcher's mitt

Pitcher's glove

Pitchers drive towards home by pushing off the pitching rubber with their back foot

ROCKET MAN
The only pitcher with five Cy Young Awards, and consecutive pitching Triple Crowns (wins, earned run average, and strikeouts) in 1997–98, he struck out a major-league record 20 batters in one game twice. With unmatched competitive fire and a great fastball, Roger Clemens has taken his place among pitching's all-time greats in his 16 seasons with the Red Sox, Blue Jays, and Yankees.

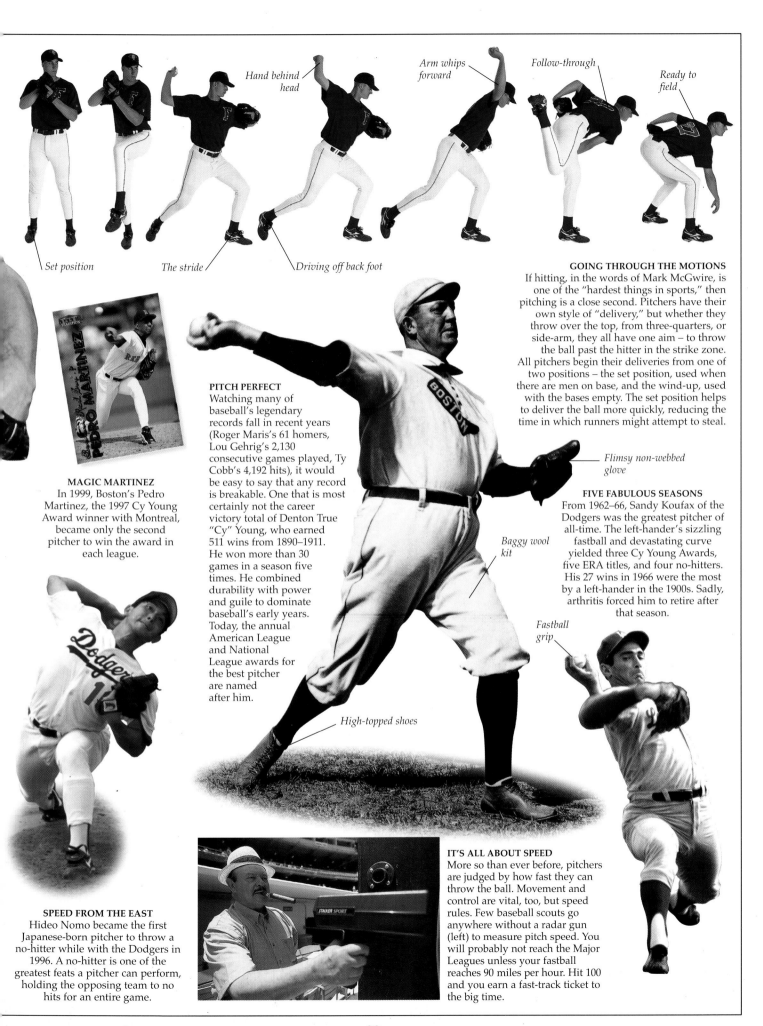

Hand behind head

Arm whips forward

Follow-through

Ready to field

Set position

The stride

Driving off back foot

GOING THROUGH THE MOTIONS

If hitting, in the words of Mark McGwire, is one of the "hardest things in sports," then pitching is a close second. Pitchers have their own style of "delivery," but whether they throw over the top, from three-quarters, or side-arm, they all have one aim – to throw the ball past the hitter in the strike zone. All pitchers begin their deliveries from one of two positions – the set position, used when there are men on base, and the wind-up, used with the bases empty. The set position helps to deliver the ball more quickly, reducing the time in which runners might attempt to steal.

MAGIC MARTINEZ
In 1999, Boston's Pedro Martinez, the 1997 Cy Young Award winner with Montreal, became only the second pitcher to win the award in each league.

PITCH PERFECT
Watching many of baseball's legendary records fall in recent years (Roger Maris's 61 homers, Lou Gehrig's 2,130 consecutive games played, Ty Cobb's 4,192 hits), it would be easy to say that any record is breakable. One that is most certainly not the career victory total of Denton True "Cy" Young, who earned 511 wins from 1890–1911. He won more than 30 games in a season five times. He combined durability with power and guile to dominate baseball's early years. Today, the annual American League and National League awards for the best pitcher are named after him.

Flimsy non-webbed glove

FIVE FABULOUS SEASONS
From 1962–66, Sandy Koufax of the Dodgers was the greatest pitcher of all-time. The left-hander's sizzling fastball and devastating curve yielded three Cy Young Awards, five ERA titles, and four no-hitters. His 27 wins in 1966 were the most by a left-hander in the 1900s. Sadly, arthritis forced him to retire after that season.

Baggy wool kit

Fastball grip

High-topped shoes

SPEED FROM THE EAST
Hideo Nomo became the first Japanese-born pitcher to throw a no-hitter while with the Dodgers in 1996. A no-hitter is one of the greatest feats a pitcher can perform, holding the opposing team to no hits for an entire game.

IT'S ALL ABOUT SPEED
More so than ever before, pitchers are judged by how fast they can throw the ball. Movement and control are vital, too, but speed rules. Few baseball scouts go anywhere without a radar gun (left) to measure pitch speed. You will probably not reach the Major Leagues unless your fastball reaches 90 miles per hour. Hit 100 and you earn a fast-track ticket to the big time.

Catching

THE HARDEST WORKING PLAYER on a baseball team is the catcher. Squatting behind the home plate for nine innings, he must catch everything a pitcher throws past a hitter, has to endure being hit by foul tips and bats, and be ready to fire perfect throws to catch would-be base stealers. Occasionally, he must deal with charging runners, who plough into him like an American football player, or soothe a pitcher's shattered ego after a home run. The great Yankee manager Casey Stengel summed up the importance of the catcher when he said, "You've got to have a catcher. Otherwise the ball will roll all the way back to the backstop."

Yogi Berra

On tag plays, catchers often remove their masks for better visibility

PLAY AT THE PLATE!
One of baseball's most exciting plays occurs when ball and runner arrive at home plate at the same time. The catcher must block the plate and tag the runner. Here Ivan Rodriguez, baseball's best catcher, does just that. Rodriguez also excels at picking off base runners with a throwing arm renowned as one of the best ever.

JUST LIKE THE PROS
Playing catcher in a youth baseball league is just as gruelling as in the pros. Like their Major League role models, young catchers wear all the protective gear available, including mask, helmet, chest protector, shin guards, and protective box. It sometimes takes young players a while to adjust to the gear, but after a few foul tips, they will find it is worth the effort.

Detachable throat protector

Extra-long youth chest protector

Shin guards with knee cups

CAMPY
After eight seasons in the African American Leagues, Roy Campanella joined the Brooklyn Dodgers in 1948 and redefined the catching position. Combining power at the plate with great catching skills, "Campy" won three MVP awards in the 1950s. Sadly, a 1958 car accident left him partially paralyzed. However, he remained close to the game and was one of baseball's most beloved figures until his death in 1993.

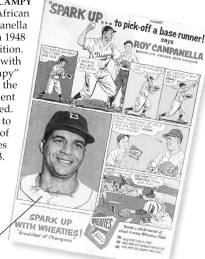

"SPARK UP... to pick-off a base-runner!" says ROY CAMPANELLA BROOKLYN DODGER STAR CATCHER

SPARK UP WITH WHEATIES! "Breakfast of Champions"

Campanella in 1950s cereal advert

FROM ICE TO DIAMOND
Most catcher's equipment has changed only in materials rather than form. The iron-barred catcher's mask of today looks much like that used in the 1930s. However, a recent innovation is changing that. Inspired by masks used by ice hockey goalies, catcher Charlie O'Brien helped design this model, which allows for more protection and greater visibility.

Elastic strap

CATCHING WITH A PILLOW
Early catcher's mitts (right) were little more than round leather pillows with space for the hand to fit into the back. The pocket was developed over time by catching the ball. There was little or no hinge or webbing. Most catchers needed to use both hands to catch. Modern gloves (opposite, top right) have made catching safer by letting catchers use only one hand.

Very small webbing area

Pocket formed at centre over time

30

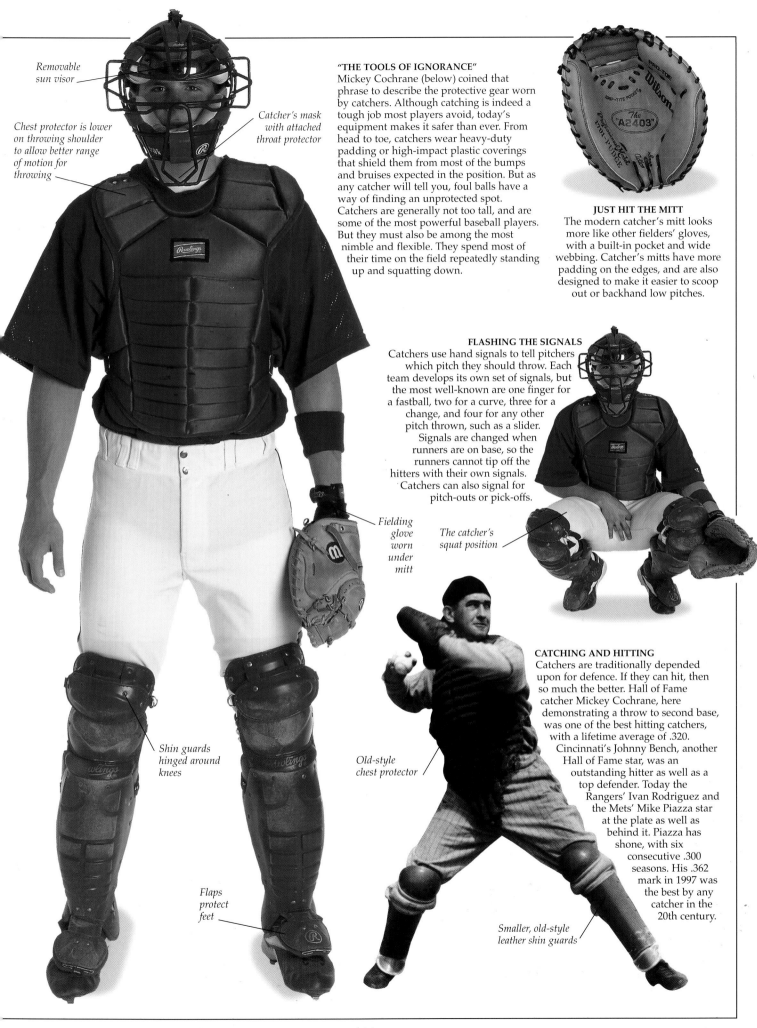

Removable sun visor

Chest protector is lower on throwing shoulder to allow better range of motion for throwing

Catcher's mask with attached throat protector

"THE TOOLS OF IGNORANCE"

Mickey Cochrane (below) coined that phrase to describe the protective gear worn by catchers. Although catching is indeed a tough job most players avoid, today's equipment makes it safer than ever. From head to toe, catchers wear heavy-duty padding or high-impact plastic coverings that shield them from most of the bumps and bruises expected in the position. But as any catcher will tell you, foul balls have a way of finding an unprotected spot. Catchers are generally not too tall, and are some of the most powerful baseball players. But they must also be among the most nimble and flexible. They spend most of their time on the field repeatedly standing up and squatting down.

JUST HIT THE MITT

The modern catcher's mitt looks more like other fielders' gloves, with a built-in pocket and wide webbing. Catcher's mitts have more padding on the edges, and are also designed to make it easier to scoop out or backhand low pitches.

FLASHING THE SIGNALS

Catchers use hand signals to tell pitchers which pitch they should throw. Each team develops its own set of signals, but the most well-known are one finger for a fastball, two for a curve, three for a change, and four for any other pitch thrown, such as a slider. Signals are changed when runners are on base, so the runners cannot tip off the hitters with their own signals. Catchers can also signal for pitch-outs or pick-offs.

Fielding glove worn under mitt

The catcher's squat position

CATCHING AND HITTING

Catchers are traditionally depended upon for defence. If they can hit, then so much the better. Hall of Fame catcher Mickey Cochrane, here demonstrating a throw to second base, was one of the best hitting catchers, with a lifetime average of .320. Cincinnati's Johnny Bench, another Hall of Fame star, was an outstanding hitter as well as a top defender. Today the Rangers' Ivan Rodriguez and the Mets' Mike Piazza star at the plate as well as behind it. Piazza has shone, with six consecutive .300 seasons. His .362 mark in 1997 was the best by any catcher in the 20th century.

Shin guards hinged around knees

Old-style chest protector

Flaps protect feet

Smaller, old-style leather shin guards

Infield and outfield

Eyes on the hitter at all times

IN DEFENCE, A BASEBALL TEAM has two main parts, infield and outfield. The four players who play near the bases form the infield. (The pitcher and catcher are officially part of the infield.) The three players who play out beyond the bases are the outfield. Each of the four infield positions – first base, second base, shortstop, and third base – has a special area of responsibility as well as skills particular to that area. The three outfield spots – left field, centre field, and right field – are more similar. Each covers about one-third of the outfield. But whatever their area of expertise, all of these players have one job when the ball is put into play – to get the runners out and stop runs from being scored. Whether that means a second baseman gathering in a routine ground ball, a centre fielder camping under a "can of corn" (easy) fly ball, or a shortstop catching the ball and firing it back across the diamond from his knees, infielders and outfielders work together to stop the opposing team.

Right hand will cover ball in glove, then remove for throw

Keep glove spread wide to "scoop" grounders

It is important to stay on the balls of your feet

THE WIZARD OF OZ
Few players in recent years have been as spectacular in the field as shortstop Ozzie Smith, who played for the Padres and Cardinals from 1978–96. His range, his ability to go down and come up throwing, and his stunning dives made him into one of the best defensive players ever in the most important defensive position.

Smith won 13 Gold Gloves from 1980-92

A CANNON IN RIGHT
Right fielders normally have the strongest throwing arm on a team because they have to make the longest throws, from deep in right field to third base. Dodgers right fielder Raul Mondesi shows how outfielders charge at the ball and use their momentum to help make their throws travel further. Mondesi has won two Gold Gloves, thanks partly to one of the game's strongest and most accurate arms.

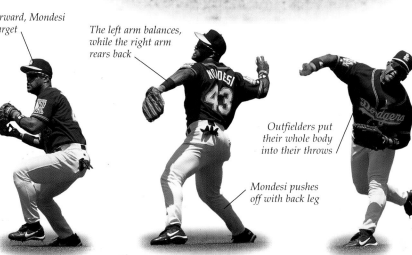

Running forward, Mondesi sights his target

The left arm balances, while the right arm rears back

Outfielders put their whole body into their throws

Mondesi pushes off with back leg

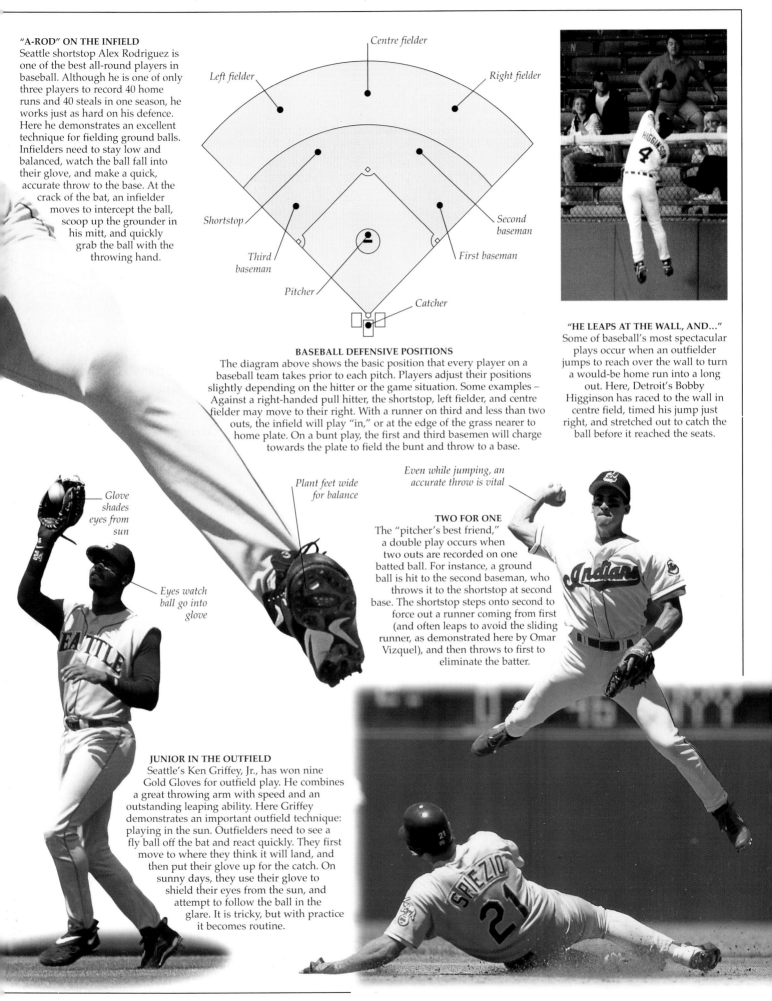

"A-ROD" ON THE INFIELD
Seattle shortstop Alex Rodriguez is one of the best all-round players in baseball. Although he is one of only three players to record 40 home runs and 40 steals in one season, he works just as hard on his defence. Here he demonstrates an excellent technique for fielding ground balls. Infielders need to stay low and balanced, watch the ball fall into their glove, and make a quick, accurate throw to the base. At the crack of the bat, an infielder moves to intercept the ball, scoop up the grounder in his mitt, and quickly grab the ball with the throwing hand.

Centre fielder

Left fielder

Right fielder

Shortstop

Second baseman

Third baseman

First baseman

Pitcher

Catcher

BASEBALL DEFENSIVE POSITIONS
The diagram above shows the basic position that every player on a baseball team takes prior to each pitch. Players adjust their positions slightly depending on the hitter or the game situation. Some examples – Against a right-handed pull hitter, the shortstop, left fielder, and centre fielder may move to their right. With a runner on third and less than two outs, the infield will play "in," or at the edge of the grass nearer to home plate. On a bunt play, the first and third basemen will charge towards the plate to field the bunt and throw to a base.

"HE LEAPS AT THE WALL, AND…"
Some of baseball's most spectacular plays occur when an outfielder jumps to reach over the wall to turn a would-be home run into a long out. Here, Detroit's Bobby Higginson has raced to the wall in centre field, timed his jump just right, and stretched out to catch the ball before it reached the seats.

Glove shades eyes from sun

Plant feet wide for balance

Even while jumping, an accurate throw is vital

Eyes watch ball go into glove

TWO FOR ONE
The "pitcher's best friend," a double play occurs when two outs are recorded on one batted ball. For instance, a ground ball is hit to the second baseman, who throws it to the shortstop at second base. The shortstop steps onto second to force out a runner coming from first (and often leaps to avoid the sliding runner, as demonstrated here by Omar Vizquel), and then throws to first to eliminate the batter.

JUNIOR IN THE OUTFIELD
Seattle's Ken Griffey, Jr., has won nine Gold Gloves for outfield play. He combines a great throwing arm with speed and an outstanding leaping ability. Here Griffey demonstrates an important outfield technique: playing in the sun. Outfielders need to see a fly ball off the bat and react quickly. They first move to where they think it will land, and then put their glove up for the catch. On sunny days, they use their glove to shield their eyes from the sun, and attempt to follow the ball in the glare. It is tricky, but with practice it becomes routine.

33

Batting

MARK McGWIRE said it for all players; hitting a baseball is the single most difficult feat in sport. The greatest hitters – or batters, the terms are interchangeable – only succeed about three times out of ten. A basketball player with that success rate would be out of a job; a field-goal kicker would not make the American football team. But batting is so hard to do well that .300 is the gold standard. In less than a third of a second, batters must decide to swing, begin their swing, and then – another tiny fraction of a second later – somehow connect a rounded bat with a wildly spinning round ball that is flying towards them at speeds that can reach more than 90 mph (145 kph). It is hard to do, but when it is done well, it is a singularly thrilling moment.

Ready to hit

Shoulder turn begins

Eyes on the ball

Wrists turn over

Full follow-through

IT SURE *LOOKS* EASY

This sequence of photos shows proper, classic hitting form. However, each player adapts this basic form to his or her needs and particular abilities. Some players will begin the swing with the bat higher or lower, or will take a short or long step with their front foot. The keys to a successful swing, though, are the same no matter what style a batter uses: consistency, keeping the eyes on the ball, and remaining smooth and quick throughout. Put all these things together, swing at the right pitch, and a hit is often the result.

Cobb played in the days before batting helmets

THE GEORGIA PEACH

Hall of Fame outfielder Ty Cobb held his hands several inches apart on the bat, a style that no one has successfully imitated. No one could match his talent, either. Cobb (Detroit, 1905-1928) used that odd style to compile a Major League record .366 lifetime average and 4,192 hits, the second highest of all time.

JUNIOR

A long, looping, upper-cut swing would spell disaster for most hitters. For Seattle Mariners centrefielder Ken Griffey, Jr., that stroke has spelled power. "Junior" reached 350 career home runs faster than any player in Major League history.

Like many players today, Griffey wears high-top cleats

OH, WHAT A HITTER

The major leagues are not the only place to find great hitters. Sadaharu Oh of the Tokyo Giants used his unusual batting style –lifting his right leg as he strode into the pitch –to hit an international record 868 career home runs in more than 3,000 fewer at-bats than major league career leader Hank Aaron.

Bat cocked toward pitcher

Gwynn demonstrates "hitting off the front foot"

High kick with front leg

34

Eyes on the ball

Firm, but not tight, grip

While Gwynn has powerful legs, his hands are the key to his success

"THE GREATEST HITTER WHO EVER LIVED"
This sequence (from top left) shows the form of Ted Williams, the Red Sox outfielder whose childhood dream was to be the greatest hitter of all time. His dream came true. Williams recorded a lifetime average of .344 with 521 home runs, even though he gave up five seasons to military service. Combining power, average, and an unerring eye, the "Splendid Splinter" could hit flat-out.

THE BEST IN THE GAME...TODAY
San Diego's sweet-swinging outfielder Tony Gwynn is the only active player in the career batting average all-time top 20. He is an eight-time National League batting champion, had more than 200 hits in five different seasons, and has hit over .300 every year since 1983. Gwynn has nearly perfect form at the plate, and his quick wrists allow him to be as adept at pulling the ball as he is "going the other way" – that is, hitting an outside pitch to left field, which is the other way for a lefthander. In 1998, he became the 21st player to reach 3,000 hits in his career.

Youth league face mask

Fingers cradle bat lightly to let bat "give" with the pitch

Hips and shoulders square to face pitcher

FIT LIKE A GLOVE
Whilst old-timers such as Cobb and Williams would have no use for them, batting gloves are essential for all but a handful of today's players. The leather and nylon gloves give players a more secure grip on the bat.

Ventilated for comfort

TRI-CURVE

franklin

Velcro-fastening wrists

LAY ONE DOWN, KID
A special type of hit is called the "bunt." The batter pushes the pitch softly so that it stays between the pitcher's mound and home plate. The batter is usually put out on a "sacrifice" bunt, but the runners on base advance.

Base running

ONCE A BATTER reaches base, he or she becomes a base runner. Being a good base runner is as important as being a good hitter. If you cannot make your way around the bases to score, it does not matter how often you get on base. Base runners advance from base to base when their team-mates put the ball into play. They can also advance by stealing a base or during a passed ball or wild pitch scenario, which is when a pitch gets past the catcher. Every base runner has one ultimate goal – to step onto home plate and score a run for the team. A base runner must always be alert to the situation – how many outs are there? What is the count? What is the score? Who is pitching? Where are the fielders? All these variables change with every pitch, so concentration is as important to a base runner as speed and technique.

Home plate umpire in position to make the call

SPEED DEMON
Cleveland's Kenny Lofton is one of baseball's best base stealers, having led the American League five times in steals. Stealing bases – running as the pitch is thrown to the plate and reaching the next base safely – is a huge offensive advantage for a team. It disrupts a pitcher's timing and sets up runners to score.

Lofton is one of baseball's fastest players

A good jump is crucial to a base stealer

HE'S OUT!
One of the hardest things for young players to learn is one of baseball's most unique skills: sliding. When running hard towards a base, sliding on the dirt is the only way to safely stop momentum and keep from going past the base. A safe slide has the head up, the top leg pointed towards the base, and the bottom leg tucked under.

Runner diving back to first

Fielder in good position to make tag

Players slide on their thighs

Batting glove

Until Jackie Robinson joined the Brooklyn Dodgers in 1947, no black man had ever played Major League baseball. For decades, racism kept thousands of great athletes out of the game until the courageous Robinson broke the barrier. Demonstrating incredible inner strength to confront outright bigotry, and fantastic baseball skills – most notably his speed and daring on the base paths – Robinson led the way.

Robinson stole home 19 times in his career

PICK-OFF PLAY

These young players are demonstrating a pick-off play at first base. One way that pitchers keep potential base stealers from getting too big a lead is to throw to first instead of to home. A good pick-off move can sometimes catch a runner napping, and the first baseman can make the tag for the out.

Books about Robinson from the 1940s and 1950s

THE BEST KIND OF RUNNING

Devon White of the Los Angeles Dodgers demonstrates every player's favourite kind of base running – the home run trot. When the ball leaves the park, players enjoy a more leisurely trip around the bases. Only a real attention seeker does anything other than a simple jog.

Base anchored to ground

Hands reach for base

Back foot on base

THE MAN OF STEALS

Rickey Henderson, here demonstrating his trademark head first slide, is baseball's all-time leader in stolen bases, with a career total of more than 1,300 (more than 400 more than Lou Brock in second place). Henderson has led the American League in steals 12 times, and in 1982 he set the single-season record with 130 while with Oakland. Henderson's speed, power, and game-saving hitting have made him into perhaps the greatest lead-off hitter in baseball history.

Hey, Blue!

Baseball is a game of rules, and the people responsible for enforcing those rules are called umpires. Umpires determine, or "call," whether a pitch is a ball or strike. They also decide whether base runners are safe or out, and whether a batted ball is foul or fair. In the Major Leagues, four umpires are used during normal season games, six in the play-offs and World Series. One of the four "umps" works behind the home plate, while the others are stationed at each of the three bases. At lower levels of baseball, anything from one to four umpires are used. Umpires have a tough job. Baseball is a fast-moving game, so umps have to make split-second decisions that can mean victory or defeat for one team or the other. Why "Hey, Blue"? Although baseball umpires appear to be wearing black, their kits are usually dark navy blue. So whatever their real names might be, all umpires will respond to the name "Blue."

OLD-TIME GEAR
Until the 1970s, home plate umpires wore a large chest protector outside their coat. This example from the 1930s was made from heavy leather. It was bulky and difficult to manage. Today's umpires wear thinner, lighter equipment under their kit shirts.

THE BRUSH OFF
Umpires need a clean, clear view of the home plate. The home plate umpire carries a small brush (an older example is pictured) to wipe off the plate periodically. Umpires always turn their back to the field before bending down to do their dusting.

Thumb wheel

KEEPING TRACK
All umpires carry hand-held "indicators" (older model, left; newer version, right) that help them keep track of the number of outs, balls, strikes, and innings. While fans consult the scoreboard for this information, the umpires have the final say.

Umpires have shirt numbers, too

THE RHUBARB
Every judgment called by an umpire upsets at least one of the two teams in the game. If a team's manager is especially upset, he may come on to the field to argue with the umpire. This might be a simple discussion – as here with the Yankees' manager Joe Torre – or a hat-flinging, dust-kicking, nose-to-nose screaming contest. Managers and players are automatically dismissed for arguing about balls and strikes.

Many managers wear trainers, not baseball spikes.

Indicating a dismissal

Dark blue shirt

Grey trousers

YOU'RE OUTTA HERE!
When an umpire decides that a player or manager has argued too much or has stepped beyond the bounds of sportsmanship, the umpire dismisses the manager or player from the game. The dismissed person must leave the dugout and return to the clubhouse. The leagues may also impose fines or additional suspensions in cases of particularly bad sportsmanship.

Signal for a strike

Sun visor

Shoulder pads protect ump from foul tips

Face mask

Chest protector is under shirt

Ball bag

Steel-toed shoes

BEHIND THE PLATE
The home plate umpire has the toughest job on an umpiring crew. He has to make split-second decisions on whether a pitch is a ball or strike, must judge any bunts fair or foul, and must make calls on close plays at the plate. Each home plate umpire develops his own personal style for calling strikes. Some are subtle, some are loud and dramatic. Also, like a catcher, the home plate umpire wears protective equipment, including a chest protector, face mask, shin guards, and heavy shoes.

HE'S IN THERE!
This umpire shows he has called the runner "safe" by spreading his arms wide. Early pro umpires did not use hand signals. When a deaf pro player named "Dummy" Hoy could not hear the umpire's vocal calls, a system of signals was developed to help him. The signals were then used for every player.

HE'S OUT!
Like home plate umpires, with their personal strike calls, base umpires develop their own unique methods for calling a player "out." This college baseball umpire demonstrates the classic "punch-out" style after the fielder has applied the tag to the runner. Other umps use an outstretched thumb on one hand, or form an "L" with their arm.

FAIR OR FOUL?
Umpires at first and third base decide whether a batted ball is fair or foul. This umpire is indicating a fair ball by pointing towards fair territory. The ball must hit the ground inside the white line to be a fair ball.

Cards and statistics

BASEBALL WITHOUT STATISTICS would be like a chocolate milkshake without chocolate. The thousands of numbers that swirl around baseball like confetti are the life-blood of the game. Statistics allow fans to compare players of today and yesterday – to marvel at 500 home runs or 300 wins, or argue whether Roger Clemens could out-pitch Walter Johnson, or to support a claim that Jackie Robinson was better than Joe Morgan. Baseball has stats for everything from pitching and hitting to base running. You might not ever need to know how well a player hits left-handers during night games in June with less than two outs, but it is possible to find the answer to this and other queries if you really want to. One of the ways that fans have enjoyed seeing all this information is on baseball cards. These little rectangles of cardboard have helped fans keep track of their heroes since the pro game began in the 1870s. Although every sport has cards now, baseball had them first.

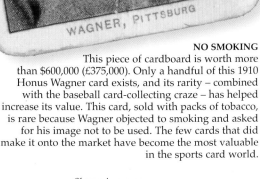

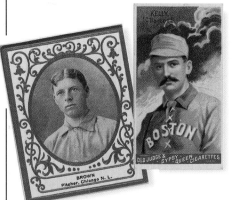

EARLY CARDBOARD HEROES
The card on the left features ace pitcher Mordecai "Three-Finger" Brown (1903–16), who finished his career with a 2.06 career ERA, third-lowest of all time. (A childhood accident cost him parts of two fingers.) On the right is Michael "King" Kelly, who was, until Babe Ruth came along, the most famous baseball player in America. He played for four National League teams from 1878–93, earned the highest salary of the day, and had a famous song composed in his honour – "Slide, Kelly, Slide."

NO SMOKING
This piece of cardboard is worth more than $600,000 (£375,000). Only a handful of this 1910 Honus Wagner card exists, and its rarity – combined with the baseball card-collecting craze – has helped increase its value. This card, sold with packs of tobacco, is rare because Wagner objected to smoking and asked for his image not to be used. The few cards that did make it onto the market have become the most valuable in the sports card world.

Robinson actually played first and second base, not outfield

Shown in pre-game warm-up gear

AN AMERICAN HERO
In 1947, Jackie Robinson not only became the first African-American player in Major League history, he also became the first black player with a baseball card. He became an instant hero for black fans everywhere, and this card was one way that his fans could carry their hero with them. In later years, as the importance of his career became more apparent, Robinson memorabilia became popular among collectors. New items were produced in 1997 for the fiftieth anniversary of his historic first season.

Signature printed on card

GETTING FANCY
As printing technologies have evolved, card designs have become wilder. Today's cards often include embossed letters, gold leaf lettering, holograms, day-glo inks, or sparkling paper. This Topps card of Kirby Puckett – who was one of baseball's most popular players until an eye ailment forced him to retire in 1995 – shows another modern trend, special sets. This All-Star set joins rookie sets, award-winner sets, superstar sets, and many others that helped fuel a boom in card collecting. Dozens of companies produce millions of cards every year, making the chances of finding a rare one pretty rare indeed.

"FATHER OF BASEBALL"

Henry Chadwick did not invent baseball, or even play it, but no one was more responsible for spreading the word about it. Beginning as a reporter in New York, he then wrote dozens of books on baseball, including the first hardback book in 1868. He helped draft rule books and edited the annual guide to the National League. Of more interest to today's fans, he invented the box score (right) as well as the system of scoring with symbols still used today.

KEEPING SCORE

Fans can follow the game by keeping score; that is, use a recognized series of symbols and numbers to record the results of each batter throughout the game. This score-card is from the 1932 World Series game in which Babe Ruth "called his shot."

HOW TO CALCULATE TWO IMPORTANT BASEBALL STATISTICS

Batting average:
Hits / At-Bats. Example:

$$\frac{125 \text{ H}}{435 \text{ AB}} = .287$$

Earned run average:
(Earned Runs x 9)/
Innings Pitched.
Example:

$$\frac{(62 \text{ ER x } 9)}{251 \text{ IP}} = 2.22$$

Some sample symbols: K for strike out, — for single, 4–3 for a ground out, second to first

Vital statistics

Name and position – in this case, 1997 NL MVP Larry Walker of the Rockies

HT: 6'3" WT: 225 BATS: L
BORN: 12/1/66
SIGNED THROUGH: 1998
RESIDES: AURORA, CO

1997	AB	HR	RBI
vs. Left	144	6	23
vs. Right	424	43	107
Home	302	20	68
Away	266	29	62
Day	261	25	57
Night	307	24	73
Grass	469	38	106
Turf	99	11	24
1st Half	309	25	68
2nd Half	259	24	62

1997	BA	OBA	SLG
vs. Left	.299	.400	.521
vs. Right	.389	.470	.788
Home	.384	.460	.709
Away	.346	.443	.733
Day	.414	.495	.835
Night	.326	.415	.622
Grass	.371	.457	.712
Turf	.343	.425	.758
1st Half	.398	.496	.741
2nd Half	.328	.397	.895

LARRY WALKER RF   13

YR	TEAM	R	H	2B	3B	HR	TB	RBI	SB	OB%	SLG%	BA
1989	Expos	4	8	0	0	0	8	4	1	.264	.170	.170
1990	Expos	59	101	18	3	19	182	51	21	.326	.434	.241
1991	Expos	59	141	30	2	16	223	64	14	.349	.458	.290
1992	Expos	85	159	31	4	23	267	93	18	.353	.506	.301
1993	Expos	85	130	24	5	22	230	86	29	.371	.469	.265
1994	Expos	76	127	44	2	19	232	86	15	.394	.587	.322
1995	Rockies	96	151	31	5	36	300	101	16	.381	.607	.306
1996	Rockies	58	75	18	4	18	155	58	18	.342	.570	.276
1997	Rockies	143	208	46	4	49	409	130	33	.452	.720	.366
MLB TOTALS		665	1100	242	29	202	2006	673	165	.374	.542	.297

Larry not only enjoyed the first 40-homer campaign of his nine-year career in 1997 but emerged as a strong contender for the National League's MVP award. He finished with career peaks in numerous offensive categories. In addition to his slugging, Larry is also a good base runner and a fine right fielder whose arm is respected by runners.

1997 FIELDING STATISTICS

	G	GS	Inn.	PO	A	E	DP	Pct.	Rng.
Walker	150	143	1235.1	230	12	5	2	.992	1.76
RF Avg	29	24	211.2	48	2	1	0	.977	2.11

Fielding stats   *Team logo*   *Manufacturer's logo*

STATS HEAVEN

The back of a player's baseball card – on most versions, as some feature other information – usually contains a wealth of statistics. Often included are the player's lifetime batting or pitching statistics, listed year-by-year, an additional note in the text describing awards or special events, and the player's vital statistics, such as height, weight, and date of birth. Fans can quickly check a player's card for almost anything they might need to know.

FIRST THING IN THE MORNING

The first place every baseball fan turns to in the morning paper is the box scores from games played the night before. Each game is summed up in a neat vertical box containing words, symbols, and numbers. Who won, who scored, who got how many hits, who pitched how many innings, and even who the umpires were. This box score shows the Padres' 10–3 victory over the Cardinals, during which St. Louis's Mark McGwire hit two home runs, the first of which was the 500th of his career.

Final score

Team, visiting team on top

Players listed in batting order, with position

Totals of each column of stats

The key stats: at-bats, runs, hits, runs batted in, walks, strike outs, batting average

McGwire's line shows two hits in four at-bats, with two RBI

Line score shows runs by inning

Padres 10, Cardinals 3

San Diego	AB	R	H	BI	BB	SO	Avg.
Veras 2b	4	2	0	0	1	1	.274
Gwynn rf	4	1	1	2	1	0	.316
RSanders lf	4	1	1	0	1	0	.298
Nevin 3b	5	1	1	2	0	0	.250
Joyner 1b	4	2	2	1	1	0	.250
Owens cf	1	0	1	2	0	0	.297
Hoffman p	4	0	0	0	0	1	.500
BDavis c	3	1	1	0	1	1	.304
Gomez ss	2	0	1	2	0	0	.240
Ashby p	1	1	1	0	0	0	.125
RRivera cf	1	0	0	0	0	0	.220
Totals	36	10	10	9	5	2	

St. Louis	AB	R	H	BI	BB	SO	Avg.
Drew cf	4	0	0	0	0	1	.261
McGee rf	4	0	0	0	0	0	.254
McGwire 1b	4	2	2	2	0	0	.279
Lankford lf	4	1	3	0	0	0	.307
Tatis 3b	3	0	0	0	1	1	.293
Renteria ss	4	0	0	1	0	1	.277
Paquette 2b	3	0	0	0	0	0	.333
Marrero c	1	0	0	0	1	0	.199
Luebbers p	0	0	0	0	0	0	.000
a-DHoward	1	0	0	0	0	0	.217
Acevedo p	0	0	0	0	0	0	.053
b-Polanco	1	0	0	0	0	0	.267
Mohler p	0	0	0	0	0	0	.000
Aybar p	0	0	0	0	0	0	.091
Totals	32	3	6	3	3	4	

San Diego   110 021 005—10 10 0
St. Louis   011 000 010— 3 6 3

a-walked for Luebbers in the 5th. b-grounded out for Acevedo in the 7th.
E-Renteria (19), Paquette (2), Marrero (5). **LOB**-San Diego 6, St. Louis 5. **2B**-Gwynn (14), Nevin (12), Hoffman (1), Lankford (21). **HR**-McGwire 2 (44) off Ashby 2. **RBIs**-Gwynn 2 (33), Nevin 2 (43), Joyner (31), Hoffman 2 (2), Gomez 2 (6), McGwire 2 (101), Renteria (44). **SB**-Veras (20), RSanders 2 (26), Owens 2 (26), Drew (9). **S**-Ashby. **SF**-Gomez. **GIDP**-Renteria.
Runners left in scoring position-San Diego 4 (RSanders 2, Joyner, BDavis); St. Louis 2 (McGee, Luebbers). **Runners moved up**-Nevin, BDavis, Paquette.
DP-San Diego 1 (Gomez, Veras and Joyner).

San Diego	IP	H	R	ER	BB	SO	NP	ERA
Ashby W, 10-5	7⅔	5	3	3	3	3	108	3.40
Hoffman S, 27	1⅓	1	0	0	0	1	19	2.89

St. Louis	IP	H	R	ER	BB	SO	NP	ERA
Luebbers L, 1-2	5	5	4	4	4	1	73	5.24
Acevedo	2	2	1	1	0	1	26	6.23
Mohler	1	0	0	0	0	0	15	4.89
Aybar	1	3	5	1	1	0	18	3.98

IBB-By Aybar (Joyner), by Ashby (Marrero).
U-Nelson, Hirschbeck, Bell, Wegner. **T**-2:47.
Tickets sold-45,106.

Various events in game are in bold

Player who did it and new season total. This shows Gwynn with 2 RBI, for a season total of 33

Pitcher's line scores: innings pitched, hits allowed, runs allowed, earned runs allowed, number of pitches, and earned run average for the season

Umpires' names

International baseball

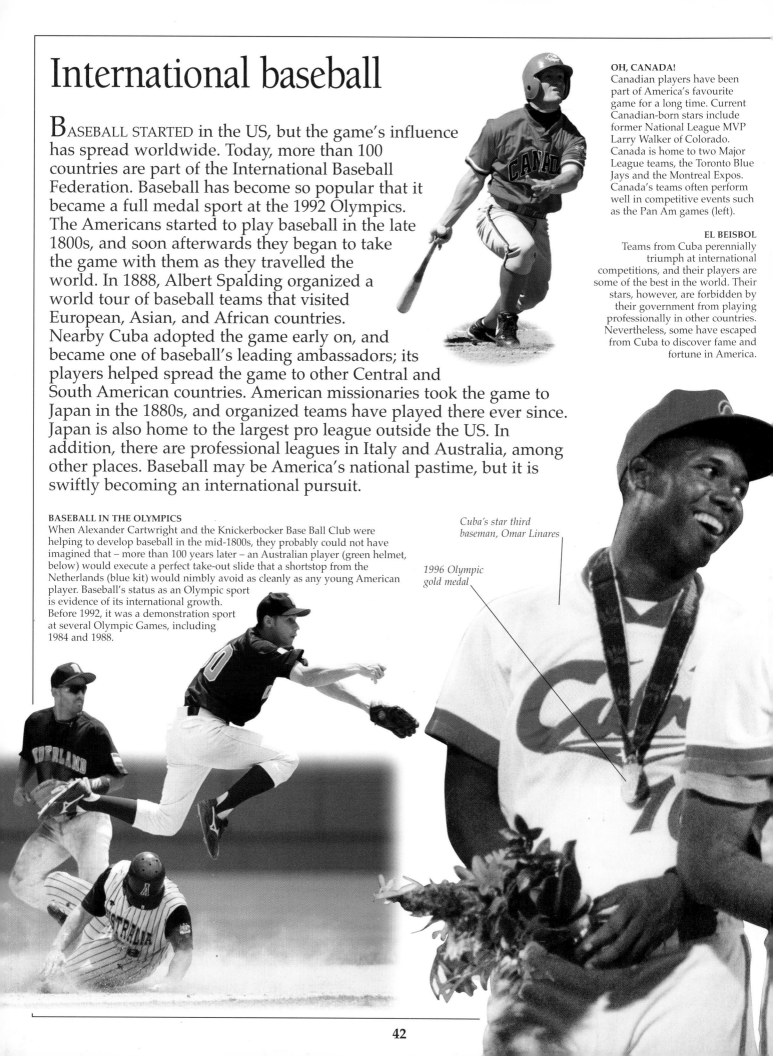

BASEBALL STARTED in the US, but the game's influence has spread worldwide. Today, more than 100 countries are part of the International Baseball Federation. Baseball has become so popular that it became a full medal sport at the 1992 Olympics. The Americans started to play baseball in the late 1800s, and soon afterwards they began to take the game with them as they travelled the world. In 1888, Albert Spalding organized a world tour of baseball teams that visited European, Asian, and African countries. Nearby Cuba adopted the game early on, and became one of baseball's leading ambassadors; its players helped spread the game to other Central and South American countries. American missionaries took the game to Japan in the 1880s, and organized teams have played there ever since. Japan is also home to the largest pro league outside the US. In addition, there are professional leagues in Italy and Australia, among other places. Baseball may be America's national pastime, but it is swiftly becoming an international pursuit.

OH, CANADA!
Canadian players have been part of America's favourite game for a long time. Current Canadian-born stars include former National League MVP Larry Walker of Colorado. Canada is home to two Major League teams, the Toronto Blue Jays and the Montreal Expos. Canada's teams often perform well in competitive events such as the Pan Am games (left).

EL BEISBOL
Teams from Cuba perennially triumph at international competitions, and their players are some of the best in the world. Their stars, however, are forbidden by their government from playing professionally in other countries. Nevertheless, some have escaped from Cuba to discover fame and fortune in America.

BASEBALL IN THE OLYMPICS
When Alexander Cartwright and the Knickerbocker Base Ball Club were helping to develop baseball in the mid-1800s, they probably could not have imagined that – more than 100 years later – an Australian player (green helmet, below) would execute a perfect take-out slide that a shortstop from the Netherlands (blue kit) would nimbly avoid as cleanly as any young American player. Baseball's status as an Olympic sport is evidence of its international growth. Before 1992, it was a demonstration sport at several Olympic Games, including 1984 and 1988.

Cuba's star third baseman, Omar Linares

1996 Olympic gold medal

Names in English

Traditional baseball kit

JAPAN'S YANKEES

Like the New York Yankees in America's Major Leagues, the Tokyo Giants have dominated Japanese baseball. The Giants, who play their games at the palatial Tokyo Dome, are by far the most popular team. They are also the most successful, having won 29 championships in the last 50 years, including a record nine consecutive titles from 1965 to 1973.

Yoshinobu Takahaski slugs a grand slam during the 1999 opening game

HOPE THEY ARE ALL GOOD CATCHERS

In 1997, after winning their third Japan Series championship in five years, the Yakult Swallows players gave their manager, Katsuya Nomura, a celebratory lift. Japan has 12 pro teams in the Central and Pacific Leagues that play a 130-game season in the spring and summer. Baseball has been played in Japan since the late 1800s.

Kit features Mexican national colours of red and green

VIVA MEXICO!

Mexico's pro baseball has almost as long a tradition as the American game. Since the 1930s, American pros have spent the winter in Mexico, improving their game against top competitors. A pro league continues today, with national all-star teams (left) performing well at international tournaments. In addition, many Mexican-born players compete in the Major Leagues, including Colorado Rockies third baseman Vinny Castilla.

Cuban player Orestes Kindelan

Flowers and laurels given to winners

COUNTRY TO COUNTRY

The United States and Cuba maintain a decades-long diplomatic separation. But in the summer of 1999, the two countries came face to face on the baseball field. For the first time, a Major League team, the Baltimore Orioles, travelled to Havana to play the Cuban national team. In return, the Cubans played at Baltimore's Camden Yards. Before the first game, Orioles star Cal Ripken, Jr., and Cuban superstar Omar Linares enjoyed a little player-to-player international relations.

The African American Leagues

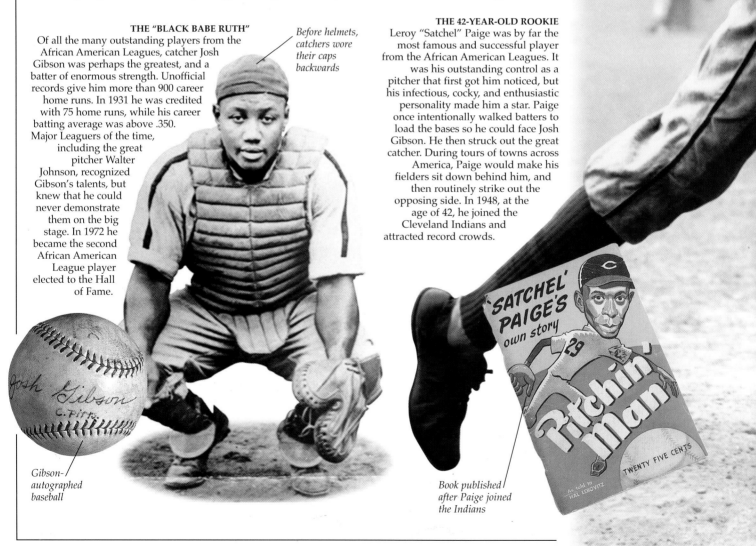

FROM ITS EARLIEST DAYS, pro baseball forbade African-Americans from taking part. Whist such behaviour would be scorned – not to mention illegal – today, the racist attitudes of that era allowed such discrimination to exist. However, although black players could not compete in the Major Leagues, nothing was going to stop them from playing the game. As early as the 1870s, all-black amateur teams were competing in the Northeast. By the turn of the century, black pro teams began to be formed, and new leagues evolved soon afterwards. These leagues as they were known, contained some of the greatest players of the century – players whose skills, most observers felt, would have made them Major League legends. The heyday of the African American Leagues came in the 1930s and 1940s, when about a dozen teams (including the Birmingham Black Barons, hat upper left) played in front of packed houses in major cities throughout the Northeast and Midwest. Finally, in 1947, Jackie Robinson became the first black player this century to play in the Majors. The African American Leagues slowly began to die out as black players took their rightful place as part of the American game.

THE "BLACK BABE RUTH"

Of all the many outstanding players from the African American Leagues, catcher Josh Gibson was perhaps the greatest, and a batter of enormous strength. Unofficial records give him more than 900 career home runs. In 1931 he was credited with 75 home runs, while his career batting average was above .350. Major Leaguers of the time, including the great pitcher Walter Johnson, recognized Gibson's talents, but knew that he could never demonstrate them on the big stage. In 1972 he became the second African American League player elected to the Hall of Fame.

Before helmets, catchers wore their caps backwards

Gibson-autographed baseball

THE 42-YEAR-OLD ROOKIE

Leroy "Satchel" Paige was by far the most famous and successful player from the African American Leagues. It was his outstanding control as a pitcher that first got him noticed, but his infectious, cocky, and enthusiastic personality made him a star. Paige once intentionally walked batters to load the bases so he could face Josh Gibson. He then struck out the great catcher. During tours of towns across America, Paige would make his fielders sit down behind him, and then routinely strike out the opposing side. In 1948, at the age of 42, he joined the Cleveland Indians and attracted record crowds.

Book published after Paige joined the Indians

THE FASTEST MAN IN SPIKES
Paige, a teammate of James "Cool Papa" Bell, claimed that Bell was so fast "he could switch off the light and be in bed before the room got dark." Bell used his speed and great batting technique to make his name in the African American Leagues from 1922-46. He joined the Hall of Fame in 1991.

Paige was elected to the Baseball Hall of Fame in 1971

Bell played for the Monarchs, Grays, Crawfords, and five other African American League teams

Baggy wool trousers

TOP TEAMS
Along with the Homestead Grays – who won a record nine consecutive league titles from 1937-45 – the Pittsburgh Crawfords (below) were among the African American Leagues' greatest teams. Three of the four players pictured here – Oscar Charleston and Josh Gibson on the left and Judy Johnson on the right – are in the Baseball Hall of Fame. Charleston in particular combined speed, defence, and hitting at the highest level of skill. New York Giants manager John McGraw called him the best player in the game, black or white.

A child's game

At least once every season, you hear a major league player say, "I sometimes can't believe it. I'm getting paid to play a kid's game." Although baseball did not start with children, they are at the base of the game's support. Millions of boys and girls around the world play baseball, either in organized leagues with teams and kits, or with their friends in the garden, park, or street. Players at the highest levels are doing the same things they did when they were children – hitting, pitching, and catching. Children are also tremendous fans of baseball. Visit any Major League park and you will see hundreds of young people cheering on their heroes or crowding around them afterwards for autographs. Baseball may be a game for everyone, but deep down it is a game for children.

SMALL PLAYERS... BIG-TIME ACTION
Children play baseball with as much heart and excitement as their Major League heroes. This play at the plate from the 1999 Little League World Series (won by Japan) looks as if it could have come from a big league game. Both the catcher and the player sliding are demonstrating great form.

MY HERO
Yankees second baseman Chuck Knoblauch (number 11) seems to be telling this young player, "Someday, maybe you, too, can play at Yankee Stadium." These members of the the Japanese champions and American runners-up of the 1999 Little League World Series were honoured on the field before a Yankees game.

Team logo

Baseball cap

Aluminium bat

JUST LIKE THE PROS
Baseball at most youth levels is very similar to that played in the Major Leagues. This pitcher from a Santa Barbara, California, Pony League team shows the same form that he sees the big leaguers use on TV. This transfer of the game from old to young helps maintain baseball's popularity.

Batting tee

Baseball trousers

TEE IT UP
Many children get their start in baseball by playing tee ball. Instead of trying to hit a pitched ball, batters take their shots at a ball placed on a batting tee. After the ball is hit, play continues as in a normal game, with base running and defence. Learning a proper batting stroke without worrying about how fast the ball is approaching helps train young players so that they will be more ready to face live pitching as they get older. Tee ball is popular with both boys and girls, aged between four and eight.

Aluminum bat approved for Little League play

Chin strap

WORLD CHAMPS!
Winning pitcher Kazuki Sumiyama (centre) of Japan is greeted by his joyous team-mates after he led his team from Osaka to the 1999 Little League World Series championship. Japan defeated a team from Phenix City, Alabama. Three other teams from the US joined teams from three other international regions in the annual Series. Sumiyama's countryman Tatsuya Sugata (left) helped Japan finish second in the 1998 Series.

Batting helmet with ear flaps

GIRLS, TOO? YOU BET!
Thousands of girls take part in youth baseball leagues at all levels. Girls have appeared in the Little League World Series and have played on school teams. A few girls have played at college, too. Girls can be just as good as boys at hitting, pitching, fielding, and baserunning. Traditionally, only boys played baseball... but that has certainly changed today.

Logo of international area represented

Leather belt

Traditional baseball trousers with stirrup socks

CHAMPS FROM THE FAR EAST
The Little League World Series has been held every summer since 1954. In the beginning, only US teams took part. Mexico was the first international team to win the Series in 1957. Four US teams reached the finals, along with teams from the Far East, Europe, Canada, and Central/South America. In 2000, the tournament field expands to 16 teams. The teams are all-star sides and all the players must come from one league. Teams from Taiwan have had the most success amongst the international opposition, winning 16 Series. Japan won the Series in 1999.

A BASEBALL TRADITION
The Little League World Series is wonderful fun for the players and coaches, as well as a great show of baseball talent for the fans. It is also a place to enjoy the popular hobby of collecting and trading souvenir badges (above). Badge traders gather different badges and pins from teams and leagues around the world.

Women in baseball

Some players wear visors instead of caps

No woman has ever played in a major league game. But that has not stopped millions of women and girls from taking part in baseball. From little girls starting out in tee ball to a handful of professional women's baseball teams, there are many opportunities for girls to play the game. One of the most popular ways is softball, a form of baseball played on a smaller diamond with a bigger ball. Women and girls usually play fast-pitch softball, in which the ball is thrown underarm as fast as boys throw baseballs overarm. In the United States there are women's pro softball leagues, and many foreign countries send their women's teams to play Olympic softball. Young girls also play in organized baseball leagues, including the Little League and the Pony League. Since 1988, several girls have even appeared in the Little League World Series. In addition, women work as umpires and coaches in youth leagues.

DAISIES · Major League GIRLS BASEBALL · 1953 OFFICIAL PROGRAM and SCORE BOOK · 15¢

Softball shorts

Softball gloves are usually larger than baseball gloves

SOFTBALL SUPERSTARS

Fast-pitch softball is one way in which many girls and women take part in a sport comparable to baseball. Pitchers – such as Lisa Fernandez, who led the US to their 1996 Olympic gold medal – throw underarm at speeds reaching 80 miles per hour. The bases are only 60 feet apart, as opposed to ninety. The ball is about 40 percent bigger than a baseball, but is not, as the name of the sport implies, soft. Otherwise, softball is quite similar to baseball, with outs, strikes, balls, innings, and runs. Pitching is more dominant in softball, however, since the mound is only 45 feet from the home plate – consequently, scores are usually lower. Young girls may play youth baseball, but most play in organized softball leagues. High schools and colleges also have fast-pitch softball programmes.

NOT BAD... FOR A GIRL

In 1931, Jackie Mitchell (above) signed a pro contract with the minor league Chattanooga Lookouts. During an exhibition game, she struck out Lou Gehrig and Babe Ruth (left), but no one knows for certain how hard they tried. In any case, Mitchell never pitched in a real game. The baseball commissioner cancelled her contract on the grounds that the game was "too strenuous for women."

First baseman's glove

Long-sleeved shirt

AAGBL players wore skirts

Knee socks

STARS OF THE SILVER SCREEN

Interest in the AAGBL grew in the 1980s when former players began to appeal for more of the league's history to be included in the Hall of Fame. Their campaign helped to further development of the movie *A League of Their Own*, which featured the Rockford Peaches.

Same type of glove as male players

A LEAGUE OF THEIR OWN

In 1943 – with the Major Leagues depleted due to World War II – Chicago Cubs owner Philip Wrigley founded a professional women's softball league to generate greater fan interest. The All-American Girls Baseball League (AAGBL) began to play that year in South Bend, Indiana; Racine, Wisconsin; Rockford, Illinois; and Kenosha, Wisconsin. Nearly 200,000 fans came out to watch the games, and attendance increased a few years later when the league changed from playing softball – and pitching underarm – to baseball.

MORE TEAMS COME TO PLAY

The growth of the AAGBL continued after World War II. The Peoria Redwings joined the AAGBL in 1946 and played every season until 1951. The small midwestern city of Peoria was typical of the hometowns of the teams. The teams relied on support from small communities and avoided big-league competition.

BORDERS CRACKS THE BARRIER

In 1994, left-handed pitcher Ila Borders – the MVP of her high school team – became the first woman to win a college game. She played at Southern California College for three years and at Whittier College for one. In 1997, the publicity-minded St. Paul Saints of the independent Northern League signed Borders to a professional contract, where she became the first woman to start and win a professional baseball game. Borders later played for the Duluth-Superior Dukes. Her success helped promote the short-lived Ladies Baseball League in 1997, and the travelling Colorado Silver Bullets team in 1997-98. Women still do not play a major role in professional baseball, but it is not for the lack of trying.

Jerseys styled after women's blouses

Team logo on cap

All the managers were male

ANYTHING FOR PUBLICITY

By 1948, the AAGBL had 10 teams in midwestern towns and cities, and nearly one million fans attended games during the 1948 season. Former Major League stars such as Jimmie Foxx and Max Carey were employed to manage the teams. Although much of the publicity surrounding the league focused on the players as women, they also gained respect for their skills on the diamond. Unfortunately, as the Major Leaguers returned from the war, interest in the women's league began to die out. The AAGBL played its last season in 1954.

Stirrup socks

Shoes similar to baseball spikes

Ballparks

POETS HAVE WRITTEN about ballparks. Songs are composed in honour of baseball parks. The brilliant green grass, the contrasting brown infield, the shirt-sleeved crowd and the pastoral nature of the ball yard – all evoke feelings one does not get from a basketball arena or a gigantic football stadium. The thrill baseball fans get from that first glimpse of green as they walk through a tunnel towards their seats is unlike any other in sports. Fathers, mothers, sons, and daughters take that walk together today, just as parents and children have for decades. Even now, as new parks spring up everywhere, they are often designed to feel like the old ballparks. With the sense of history that baseball creates, a ballpark is more than just a place where two teams play; it is, as the movie said, a field of dreams.

Christy Mathewson

FAN FOR FANS
Whether a hand-held fan honouring a baseball hero or a medal made for Mother's Day (far left), there have been promotional items created for ballpark fans from baseball's earliest days. Special days are held throughout the season at which fans get everything from bats to beach towels and Beanie Babies.™

THE SEAT WHERE THEY LIVED
This is a "bleacher" seat from Crosley Field, home of the Cincinnati Reds from 1912–70. This fabled old field was demolished in 1970 and the Reds moved to the more modern, but less charming, Riverfront Stadium – now known as Cinergy Field.

Usher's cap and ID badge

HOME OF "DA BUMS"
Few cities have ever had a closer relationship with a ballpark than Brooklyn, New York had with Ebbets Field. This tiny shoebox of a stadium was home to the Dodgers from 1913 to 1957, when the team broke millions of local hearts and moved to Los Angeles. On the right field fence, clothes seller Abe Stark placed a notice that read, "Hit this sign, win free suit."

Outfield bleacher seats

Upper deck

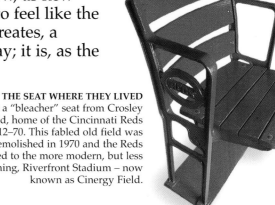

HONOURING JACKIE
In 1997, on the 50th anniversary of Jackie Robinson becoming the first African-American in the modern major leagues, Major League Baseball announced that Robinson's number 42 would be retired by every club. Every team now honours Robinson somewhere in its stadium, such as this mural in Dodger Stadium.

FRIENDLY CONFINES

One of baseball's most revered ballparks is Wrigley Field, home of the Chicago Cubs. Ivy (right) grows on its brick outfield walls. Fans can watch from the roofs of apartment buildings located behind the stadium.

Distance in feet (122 m) from home plate

ULTRA-MODERN

The Skydome, home of the Toronto Blue Jays, was the first sports stadium with a retractable roof. The large, curved portion at the top slides along tracks to cover the field and the fans in case of bad weather. Seattle's Safeco Field and Tampa's Tropicana Field also boast similar technological marvels. The Skydome has a hotel and several restaurants inside it, too.

A COSY LITTLE PARK

This aerial view of Tiger Stadium in Detroit shows how the park was squeezed into the neighbourhood. That was how the first ballparks were constructed. Compare the cramped feeling of this old ball yard, built in 1912, with the expansive design of Dodger Stadium (below). The Tigers played their last game on this field in 1999, moving to Comerica Park for the 2000 season. Some fans mourn the loss of these old ballparks (Boston's Fenway Park is now the oldest park in the Majors. It, too, opened in 1912). And while most people now agree that vast, impersonal stadiums are not the answer, fans have come out in droves to new stadiums in Baltimore, Cleveland, Arlington, and elsewhere. Why? Because they combine the best features of the old-time parks with modern amenities.

Light tower

Scoreboard

PROGRAMMES! GET YOUR PROGRAMMES!

Few fans leave a ballpark empty-handed. Concession stands, such as this one at Baltimore's Camden Yards, are located throughout the stadium and offer everything a fan could want.

Box seats

TAKE US OUT TO THE BALLPARK

This panoramic view of Dodger Stadium in Los Angeles shows how most baseball stadiums are laid out. A horseshoe of seats surrounds the field, with the bottom of the U-shape at home plate. Raised bleachers rise up beyond the outfield wall. Most fans think the best seats are behind home plate or along the baselines between the bases and home plate. But some fans always choose the cosy bleachers.

Baseball hall of fame

VISITING THE BASEBALL HALL OF FAME is like taking a walk through a history book. Located in Cooperstown, New York, the Hall of Fame contains all of the important artefacts and memorabilia from baseball's past – with more items added every year. On display at the Hall are bats used by Nap Lajoie, Babe Ruth, and Mark McGwire; balls hit by Lou Gehrig, Hank Aaron, and Sammy Sosa; caps worn by Christy Mathewson, Satchel Paige, and Roger Clemens; plus bases stolen by Ty Cobb, Lou Brock, and Rickey Henderson. There are also thousands of programmes, score-cards, posters, pennants, and souvenirs to look at. The Hall's library contains millions of photographs and important baseball records, and serves as a key resource for scholars researching the sport. The most important function of the Hall of Fame, however, is to honour the greatest players, coaches, and contributors in the game. Every year, a new class of baseball greats is admitted to the Hall, to become an inherent part of the game's legendary history.

ULTIMATE HONOUR

Whilst pro players annually strive for a World Series ring, as their careers progress they keep one eye on Cooperstown. The reward for the best players is baseball immortality in the form of a plaque, like the one below for 1999 Hall entrant George Brett. The plaque lists the player's career accomplishments, including any records and key awards. Brett played for only one team, the Kansas City Royals, during his 20-year career. But players who have represented more than one team may choose which hat they will wear on their bronze, bas-relief plaque.

THE RYAN EXPRESS

Nolan Ryan pitched in the Major Leagues for 27 seasons – the most of any player. His overpowering fastball made him a dominant force for many of those years. He is the all-time career leader in strikeouts, and set the single-season record in 1973 with 383. Ryan also threw seven no-hitters – the most by any pitcher. The above ball is now in the Hall of Fame, where Ryan was admitted in 1999.

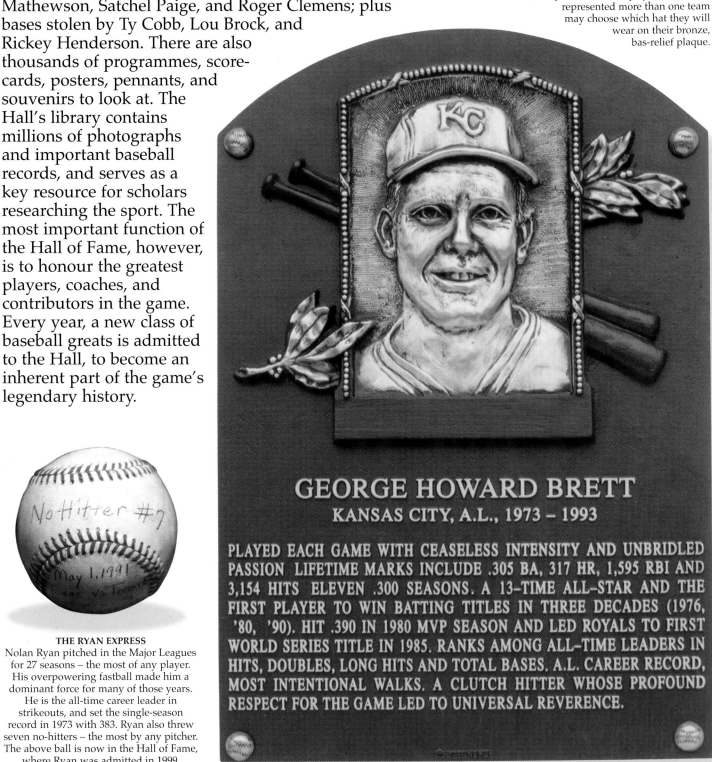

GEORGE HOWARD BRETT
KANSAS CITY, A.L., 1973 – 1993

PLAYED EACH GAME WITH CEASELESS INTENSITY AND UNBRIDLED PASSION LIFETIME MARKS INCLUDE .305 BA, 317 HR, 1,595 RBI AND 3,154 HITS ELEVEN .300 SEASONS. A 13-TIME ALL-STAR AND THE FIRST PLAYER TO WIN BATTING TITLES IN THREE DECADES (1976, '80, '90). HIT .390 IN 1980 MVP SEASON AND LED ROYALS TO FIRST WORLD SERIES TITLE IN 1985. RANKS AMONG ALL-TIME LEADERS IN HITS, DOUBLES, LONG HITS AND TOTAL BASES. A.L. CAREER RECORD, MOST INTENTIONAL WALKS. A CLUTCH HITTER WHOSE PROFOUND RESPECT FOR THE GAME LED TO UNIVERSAL REVERENCE.

Honus Wagner Grover Cleveland Alexander Tris Speaker Napoleon Lajoie George Sisler Walter Johnson

Eddie Collins Babe Ruth Connie Mack Cy Young

A GATHERING OF GREATNESS

In 1936, baseball began electing players and coaches to the Baseball Hall of Fame. The Hall itself did not open until 1939, on the alleged 100th anniversary of baseball – the anniversary was based on the now rejected theory that Abner Doubleday "invented" the game in 1839. This photograph of all the contemporary Hall of Fame members was taken at the dedication. Ty Cobb was also at the event, but missed the photograph. These players, together with long-time Philadelphia owner and manager Connie Mack, make up one of the greatest assemblies of baseball talent ever in one place.

B for Brooklyn

JACKIE'S CAP

The Hall of Fame boasts an enormous collection of baseball caps, including this one worn by Dodgers' great Jackie Robinson. The collection includes caps from every era of pro and amateur baseball. When asked, players gladly donate their caps to the Hall to commemorate a special occasion.

Classic Yankee pinstripes

1956 WORLD SERIES
AMERICAN LEAGUE VS NATIONAL LEAGUE

1956 WORLD SERIES
American League — National League

26 178A 1

SECTION BOX SEAT

ENTER AT GATE 2

MEZZANINE BOX SEAT

GAME   YANKEE STADIUM
NEW YORK YANKEES
Agent

GAME 5 ONLY
Do not detach this coupon from RAIN CHECK.

MEZZANINE BOX SEAT $10.50
TAX INCLUDED

RAIN CHECK
RETAIN THIS CHECK
Not Good If Detached
ADMIT ONE—Subject to the conditions set forth on the back hereof.
Played Under the Supervision of
FORD C. FRICK
Commissioner of BASEBALL

TICKET TO HISTORY

This 1956 World Series ticket is an example of the Hall of Fame's vast collection of written records relating to the game. Every season, the historians at the Hall add many more items to their collection of tickets, scorebooks, magazines, books, and newspaper articles.

CLASS OF 1999

The annual Hall of Fame induction ceremony is one of the great events of each baseball season. Inductees are presented in front of a crowd of thousands and give speeches broadcast nationwide thanking those who helped them reach the top. These four all-time great players were admitted to the Hall in 1999.

DIRTY DIMAGGIO

One of the great hallmarks of the artefacts fans can witness at the Hall of Fame is their authenticity. This jersey is a good example. Worn by Yankee great Joe DiMaggio, it preserves the sweat, dirt and grass stains that the "Yankee Clipper" put there himself. These artefacts aren't replicas – they are the real thing. Along with the hundreds of items on display, the Hall also carefully stores and preserves thousands of other pieces of baseball memorabilia, creating new exhibits every season that highlight different aspects of baseball's past.

Orlando Cepeda Robin Yount Nolan Ryan George Brett

World Series history

THE HISTORY OF MAJOR LEAGUE BASEBALL can be traced almost completely by following the chronicles of the World Series. The game's annual championship – played between the champions of the American and National Leagues – has become as much a part of America's calendar as the Fourth of July. The first Fall Classic, as it is sometimes called, was in 1903 (left), and it has been played every year – with one notable exception – since 1905. The exception? (see below) The 1994 World Series was cancelled during a labour dispute between players and owners. Every other year, the World Series has gone on through war and peace and everything in between. Whilst generations of baseball's greatest players have created indelible memories on the field, the consistent popularity of the World Series has helped create a colourful legacy of Series memorabilia, as shown here.

1903: Boston wins five games to three.

THE BLACK SOX

The fan who used this ticket to the 1919 World Series between the Cincinnati Reds and the Chicago White Sox witnessed one of baseball's darkest hours. Eight members of the White Sox conspired with gamblers to throw the Series to the underdog Reds. The "Black Sox," as they came to be known, were later suspended from baseball for life. One of them, "Shoeless" Joe Jackson, was one of the greatest hitters of all time. Jackson's role in the fix is debatable, but there is no doubt that the fix occurred. Baseball's pure reputation had been tarnished.

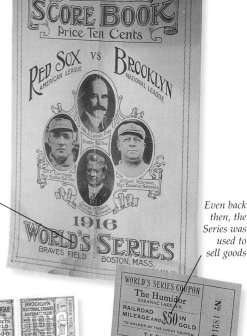

An early memorabilia version of the event's name

Even back then, the Series was used to sell goods

PINNING DOWN THE WORLD SERIES

The now-popular hobby of collecting medals commemorating major sporting events did not start with the Olympics. Medals (or pins) such as the ones below have been issued for the World Series since the first games. An example from 1913 (below) shows an early version of the name of the event, "World's Series." The members of the press covering the Series have always enjoyed special pins, such as the ribbon in the centre, issued in 1917 by the New York Giants, and the medal at the top left, issued by the American League in 1927.

From 1908, the year of the Giants' first Series appearance

Note low $5 (about £1) price for a great seat

New York Giants tie clip

Baseball made for cancelled 1994 Series

THE BABE'S SERIES DEBUT

The great Babe Ruth made his World Series debut in 1916, but he made his mark as a pitcher, not a hitter. Ruth's 14-inning, complete game, one-run victory in Game 2 proved to be the key to Boston's title. The Red Sox would win again with Ruth in 1918 for their fifth title in 15 seasons. Ruth left the next season, and Boston has not won a Series since.

THE SERIES THAT WASN'T

Disagreements between owners and players have been a part of baseball since the 1860s. The worst example of baseball labour problems came in 1994. Amid an ongoing battle over salaries, the players went on strike on August 12 that year, and they did not return until 1995. For the only time in the history of the event, the World Series was cancelled.

THE RIVALRY

For decades, the Brooklyn Dodgers and the New York Yankees were fierce derby rivals, facing each other seven times during the World Series; Brooklyn only won in 1955. The Dodgers moved to Los Angeles in 1959. In 1963, they beat the Yankees in the Series, winning in L.A. on the strength of pitcher Sandy Koufax's magical left arm.

Pennants representing
each Major League team

A TRIP TO THE WHITE HOUSE
Since baseball is America's pastime, it is only fitting that – as an annual ritual – the World Series champions pay a visit to the White House to meet the President soon after they win the title.

President Bill Clinton with manager Joe Torre of the 1998 champion Yankees

Logos of league champions

CHAMPAGNE DREAMS COME TRUE
Until recently, after the final game of each World Series, the commissioner of baseball visited the locker room of the jubilant winning team to present this trophy to the team owners and manager. Recently, to make the presentation more fan-friendly, the ceremony has moved to a stage hastily built on the field amid the celebrating players and fans. What was once a champagne-soaked party in cramped, plastic-covered quarters has become a field-spanning spectacle of fireworks, frivolity, and fun. Players race across the field to hug each other, they bring their children down from the stands and they climb on top of police horses for triumphant parades. All the while, a stadium full of fans – and millions more watching on TV – bears witness to the unbridled joy of victory.

WORLD CHAMPIONS
BALTIMORE ORIOLES
1983

*Champion's name
engraved on base*

THE MIGHTY YANKEES
The New York Yankees have dominated the World Series like no other team. The Bronx Bombers have appeared in 35 World Series and won 24 times, more than twice as many as their nearest rivals, the Athletics and the Cardinals (who have won nine Series each). The Yankees won their first World Series in 1923. Their most recent championship was in 1998 (below), when they won a record 125 games in the regular- and post-season combined. They are the only team to win four World Series in a row (1936–39), and the only team to win five in a row (1949–1953). They have won at least one title in every decade except the 1980s.

PEPSI
16 FL.

1975
WORLD
CHAMPIONS

CINCINNATI
REDS

BICENTENNIAL
JULY 4, 1976
COMMEMORATIVE
BOTTLE

DRINK OF CHAMPIONS
Most Series souvenirs are traditional, such as pennants, hats, and shirts. But there is always room for items such as this commemorative drink.

RINGING IN THE TITLE
While the World Series trophy resides in the winning team's offices, the players' symbol of victory is the World Series ring. This model, from the 1954 New York Giants, shows an early example. Recent rings are enormous, with many diamonds.

*Yankees' famous
top hat logo*

World Series heroes

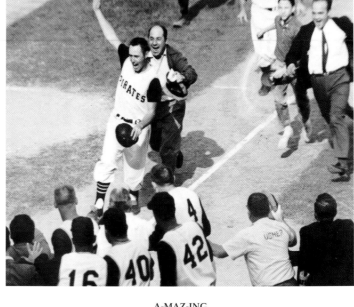

Two outs, bottom of the ninth, in the seventh game of the World Series. Your team is behind, and it is all up to you. Can you save the day? For nearly 100 years, children across America have played that scene in their minds and in their playground games. Can you make the big hit and win the Series? Can you be a hero? When the time came for the men on these pages to ask that question of themselves and face the great pressure of the World Series – whether that moment came in the bottom of the ninth or earlier – they answered, "Yes, I can!" Like the children they all once were, it was a dream come true.

A-MAZ-ING
Until 1960, no team had earned its World Series title by hitting a home run on the final swing of the Series. Then along came Bill Mazeroski. The Pirates' second baseman, known more for his outstanding fielding than his hitting, led off the bottom of the ninth with the Yankees and Pirates tied 9–9 in Game Seven. Maz slugged a home run into the left field seats for a shocking 10–9 victory over the Yankees.

PITCHER PERFECT
On baseball's biggest stage, no pitcher was ever better for one game than Don Larsen. In the fifth game of the 1956 World Series, the Yankees right-hander threw the only perfect game in World Series history, and one of only 17 such games in all of baseball since 1880. Larsen, being congratulated here by catcher Yogi Berra, faced 27 Brooklyn Dodgers and retired them all. Not one Dodger reached first base.

Larsen's career record was 81–91

THE YANKEE CLIPPER
Yankees centre fielder Joe DiMaggio never won a World Series with a homer or made a Series-winning catch. He just won. In 13 seasons (1936–51) with the Yankees, DiMaggio led the team to 10 World Series titles. His game-saving hitting (he had 30 RBI in 51 games), graceful fielding, and quiet leadership were the cornerstones to the great Yankees teams of the 1930s and 1940s. DiMaggio, who died in 1999, became an enduring symbol of the Yankees' dynasty.

GREAT GIBBY
Although it came in Game One of the 1988 World Series, and not Game Seven, a dramatic two-run homer by injured and limping Kirk Gibson in the bottom of the ninth gave the Los Angeles Dodgers the lift they needed to upset the favoured Oakland A's for the Series title.

A GREAT MAN ON AND OFF THE FIELD
In the 1971 World Series, Roberto Clemente, the pride of Puerto Rico, hit .414 while reaching base safely in all seven games. His home run in Game Seven proved decisive as the Pirates defeated the Orioles 2–1 to win the Series. Clemente's final Series appearance was bitter-sweet. Following the 1972 season, when he reached 3,000 career hits in his last game, Clemente was tragically killed in a plane crash while helping deliver supplies to earthquake victims in Nicaragua.

In 1941, DiMaggio hit safely in a record 56 consecutive games

Jackson hit 10 Series home runs, fifth most of all time

CARTER'S CLOUT

Toronto outfielder Joe Carter leaps for joy as he watches his World Series-winning homer leave the park in 1993's Game Six. The three-run blast brought the Blue Jays to victory from a run behind. They won the game 8–6 and the Series 4–2 over the Philadelphia Phillies.

MISTER OCTOBER

Few players in baseball history have craved the limelight like Reginald Martinez Jackson. Reggie Jackson earned his nickname of "Mister October" with a string of much-needed hits in World Series games for Oakland and New York. But it was in Game Six of the 1977 World Series that he carved a permanent place in baseball folklore. Jackson blasted home runs on three consecutive pitches from Dodgers hurlers. Only Babe Ruth, who did it twice, has also hit home runs three times in a Series game.

Fisk's bat

FISK AND FENWAY

Red Sox catcher Carlton Fisk ended what many call the greatest game in Series history – Game Six in 1975 – with a home run in the bottom of the twelfth inning. Fisk's homer over Fenway Park's "Green Monster" gave Boston a 7–6 victory.

Jackson had 563 home runs in his career

The home run

FOUR-BAGGER. Circuit clout. Round-tripper. Dinger. Tater. *Quadrangular*. Homer. By any name, the home run is baseball's signature moment. Smash the ball out of the yard and you render the other team helpless. There is no defence for a home run, and nothing energizes a crowd or a team like a well-timed shot to the seats. All of baseball's greatest heroes are home run hitters – the Babe, Larrupin' Lou, Old Double X, the Mick, Say-Hey Willie, Hammerin' Hank, and Big Mac. The frenzy created by Mark McGwire and Sammy Sosa as they chased history and each other throughout 1998 would not have happened if they had been chasing the record for doubles. Purists can argue that home runs are overvalued, and that players ruin their swings aiming for the fences instead of the gaps. But here is a guarantee; all of those purists are on their feet yelling along with the rest of us as a record-setting or World Series-winning home run soars through the sky into history. Back-back-back-back! Going, going, gone! Goodbye, Mr. Spalding! It might be, it could be, it is... a home run!

Aaron broke in with the Milwaukee Braves, who later moved to Atlanta

HAMMERIN' HANK
On April 8, 1974, Hank Aaron broke a record many thought was unbreakable. The Braves outfielder, shown here early in his career, hit his 715th career home run, breaking the standard set by the immortal Babe Ruth. Aaron, who finished his career in 1976 with 755 homers, suffered from racist threats as he approached Ruth's mark. But his class and talent overcame the bigotry. Sadly, Aaron remains one of the sporting world's least appreciated superstars.

No words were needed when Aaron set the record

THE SHOT HEARD 'ROUND THE WORLD
Giants outfielder Bobby Thomson hit one of baseball's most famous home runs, a three-run shot in the bottom of the ninth inning that gave the Giants the 1951 National League championship over the Brooklyn Dodgers.

Thomson earned a hug from Giants manager Leo Durocher (left)

Compare the baggy trousers worn by Aaron in 1961 with the sleek outfits of McGwire and Sosa (right)

The pressure of the assault on 60 caused Maris's hair to fall out

GOING FOR 61 IN '61
In 1961, Yankees outfielders Mickey Mantle and Roger Maris made a double assault on Ruth's single-season home run record of 60. Maris became the new home run king with his 61st homer in the final game of the season, setting a standard that would last until 1998.

ROGER MARIS

A September, 1961, knee injury ended Mantle's chase

THE MIGHTY MICK
Mickey Mantle hit 536 home runs – the eighth highest of all time. But there is more to Mantle's home run story than a number. He holds the career record for World Series home runs with 18, hitting them when his team needed them most. He holds the record for the most homers by a switch-hitter, demonstrating his power from both sides of the plate. He also hit what has been called the longest home run ever, a mammoth 172 m (565 ft) blast at Washington's Griffith Stadium in 1952. If not for his constant injury problems, Mantle may have caught up with the Babe, too.

Mantle underwent several knee surgeries

McGwire's bat is now in the Hall of Fame

Mantle's speed and Oklahoma hometown earned him the nickname – the Commerce Comet

RECORD BREAKER
With this mighty swing on September 8, 1998, Cardinals first baseman Mark McGwire hit his Major League record 62nd home run of the season, capping off a remarkable chase of the previous record of 61 set by Roger Maris in 1961. An entire nation of fans followed Big Mac's every at-bat throughout the summer as he neared the magic number. But while McGwire's moon-shot power was the cause of all the fuss (he ended the season with an amazing 70 homers), it was his class, style, and grace under pressure that made the summer of '98 so special.

Venerable Cubs logo

HOME RUN HOP
While McGwire was chasing Maris, Cubs outfielder Sammy Sosa was chasing McGwire. After hitting a record 20 home runs in June, Sosa joined McGwire as the daily focus of fans across the country. The smiling slugger from the Dominican Republic ended the 1998 season with 66 home runs, also breaking Maris's record, while gaining a new legion of fans because of his exuberant and enthusiastic approach to the game.

QUITE A NICKNAME
Frank "Home Run" Baker (far right) earned his famous nickname by reaching double digits in home runs five times, during a "dead-ball" era when teams did not hit 10 homers in a season.

McGwire wears a plastic guard on his ankle to protect against foul tips

Index

Acknowledgements

The author, Dorling Kindersley Publishing, and the Shoreline Publishing Group offer their grateful thanks for assistance in creating this book to: Rich Pilling and Paul Cunningham of Major League Baseball; W.C. Burdick of the National Baseball Hall of Fame and Library; Bob and Ed Rosato of Rosato Sports Photography; Elizabeth Daws of the Rawlings Co.; Hillerich & Bradsby; Carolyn McMahon of AP/World Wide Photos; and the marvelous memorabilia collection of David Spindel. Special thanks to Bill Pintard of the California state champion Santa Barbara Foresters for helping to arrange for players

Adam Berry and Wade Clark to pose for photographs. Additional production assistance was provided by Seth Mandelbaum.
The following books were key resources for the author. Note that all statistics in the book are current through September, 1999.
Total Baseball (Total Sports, 1999) by John Thorn, et al. This is the official encyclopedia of Major League Baseball and was the checking source for statistics.
The New Dickson Baseball Dictionary (Harcourt Brace, 1999) by Paul Dickson.
Green Cathedrals (Addison Wesley, 1992) by Philip J. Lowry.
The Series (Sporting News, 1991)

Photography Credits:
t = top; b = bottom; l = left; r = right; c = centre
Associated Press 14tl, 14bc, 15c, 15cr, 15cr, 15bc, 15br, 17tl, 24c, 29bl, 29br, 31br, 33tr, 34bl, 34bc, 34br, 34tr, 36tr, 37br, 38bl, 38br, 39tr, 39cr, 39br, 42-43 (7), 44bl, 44c, 45br, 46tr, 46cr, 47tl, 47tr, 48bl, 48tr, 49tr, 51tl, 52bl, 52c, 53bl, 53tl, 55tr, 56-57 (7), 58bl, 58tr, 59tr. **Michael Burr** 20c (5), 20b, 20t, 21c (2), 25br, 28tl (5), 29t (7), 31l, 31cr, 34tl(5), 38cr, 44tl, 47bl, 55bc. **Christie's** 40tr. **DK Publishing** 18tl. **Mike Eliason** 16cr, 18br, 19tl, 21bl, 22c, 24bl, 29bc, 30cl, 32br(3), 35br, 36bl, 37bl, 37cr, 46cr, 46bc, 50br. **Franklin Sports, Inc.,** 35bc. **Library of Congress** 10bc, 10c, 11br, 13t, 18tr, 22tl, 26bl, 29c, 45br, 59bl. **Rich Pilling/Major League Baseball**

Photos 16bc, 17r, 23br, , 30bl, 33br, 39l, 59cl. **Louis DeLuca/Major League Baseball** 27cr. **National Baseball Hall of Fame and Library** 10c, 12tl, 12bc, 19tr, 21tr, 25tr, 38tl, 41tl, 48tl, 49cl, 49tc, 53bl, 53c, 53tr. **Rawlings Co.** 21tl, 22br, 24tr, 27cl, 31tr. **Bob Rosato** 16bl, 16tr, 17bl, 18c, 27l, 28r, 30tr, 32bl, 32tr, 35l, 37cr, 50c, 59br. **David Spindel** 10tl, 11r, 12c, 12bl, 12cr, 13bl, 13br, 13cr, 14bl, 14cr, 15tr, 22cl, 22bl, 23br, 24br, 25bl, 26tr, 26cr, 26br, 27tr, 30cr, 30br, 34tr, 36tl, 37c, 38cl, 40cl(2), 40bl, 41cl, 44bl, 44br, 50tl, 50tr, 50cl, 51tr, 51br, 54tl, 54bl, 54bc, 54tr, 54cr, 54br, 55tl, 55bl, 55br, 58c, 59tl. **University of Notre Dame Libraries,** 49tl, 49br. **Wilson Sporting Goods Co.,** 23c(3).